make your own Great Earrings

make your own Great Earrings

Beads

Wire

Polymer Clay

Fabric

Found Objects

Jane LaFerla

LARK
BOOKS

ASHEVILLE, NORTH CAROLINA

ART DIRECTION AND PRODUCTION: **Chris Bryant**

COVER DESIGN: **Chris Bryant**

ILLUSTRATIONS: **Orrin Lundgren**

PHOTOGRAPHY: **Evan Bracken**

Library of Congress Cataloging-in-Publication Data

LaFerla, Jane.
    Make your own great earrings : beads, wire, polymer clay, fabric,
found objects / Jane LaFerla.—1st. ed.
      p. cm.
    Includes index.
    ISBN 1-57990-031-3 (hardcover). — ISBN 1-57990-014-3 (paper).
    1. Jewelry making. 2. Earrings. I. Title
    TT212.L34 1998
    745.594'2—dc21   97–26423
                                      CIP

10 9 8 7 6 5 4 3 2 1

First Edition

Published by Lark Books
50 College Street
Asheville, North Carolina 28801, USA

© 1998 by Lark Books

Distributed by Random House, Inc., in the United States, Canada,
  the United Kingdom, Europe, and Asia

Distributed in Australia by Capricorn Link (Australia) Pty Ltd.,
  P.O. Box 6651, Baulkham Hills Business Centre, NSW 2153, Australia

Distributed in New Zealand by Tandem Press Ltd.,
  2 Rugby Rd., Birkenhead, Auckland, New Zealand

Printed in Hong Kong

ISBN 014-3 Paper
     031-3 Hard

CONTENTS

INTRODUCTION

THIS BOOK IS DEDICATED TO UNABASHED, INSATIABLE EARRING ADDICTS. You know who you are. One pair, three pairs, a dozen are never enough. For you, earrings transcend mere personal ornamentation and become objects of passionate desire—you marvel at their good looks; you must possess them at all cost; you cry when the best ones are lost.

While others think you wear earrings solely for adornment, you know their true purpose—they're your arsenal of amulets, talismans that protect you, empower you, lift your spirits, signal moods, beliefs, and even hint at seduction. You know you can alter the course of a day, even a lifetime, by the earrings you choose to wear that morning.

Perhaps more than any other form of personal ornamentation, earrings tell your story. Rather than wear your heart on your sleeve, you dangle your inner-most life from your ear lobes for all the world to see. Just take a tour of your jewelry box.

Most of you will find a treasure chest full of tiny compartments that hold the mementos of a lifetime— next to the singular diamond studs (anniversary) are the little angels (a gift from your sister), the colorful parrots (vacation), painted macaroni (kids), grandma's opals (to remember), small, tasteful hoops and buttons (office wear), and the incredible, handcrafted, bead dangles you wear 99 percent of the time simply because they are really "you."

Now you can relax and accept the benediction found in these pages—it's perfectly respectable to be an earring fanatic. This book lets you carry your love of earrings a step further (if that's possible). Now you can indulge yourself in wild abandon while maintaining your dignity. Be proud of who your are but get to work.

By making your own great earrings, you can ease your guilt about emptying the family coffers for your ever expanding earring wardrobe. At the same time, you can have fun learning new techniques to help you create earrings that make a unique personal statement.

HOW TO USE THIS BOOK

This book allows you to explore making earrings by using a wide array of materials and easy techniques. One way to treat this book is to look at it as a sampler for investigating new how-tos with materials you've never tried. Or, you can pick a section and expand your knowledge of your chosen craft.

Whether you enjoy working with fiber, beads, metals, or polymer clay, you should be able to derive enough inspiration from the projects in this book to begin experimenting with your own designs. No matter how you approach this book, at the end of a project you'll have a pair of earrings to wear that show your flair for handcrafted work.

The beginning of each major section will give you information about specific tools, materials, and basic instructions to get started. As you work on the individual projects, you can refer to those pages as needed.

Each designer has provided step-by-step instructions for their earrings, many with easy-to-follow illustrations. While you can pick up some valuable tips by just reading through the projects, you'll have much more fun making them.

Throughout the book you'll find short pieces on earring lore and history. Read them as a way to gain a perspective on these favored adornments. You'll see why earrings have remained so popular throughout the centuries.

So let yourself go—dangles, studs or loops, wire, clay or glass, beads, baubles and bottle caps. You'll be amazed at the simple materials you can transform into a pair of earrings, and equally amazed at how easy it is to make your own great earrings. Not only will you add a new dimension to your earring wardrobe, you can share your mania with family and friends through custom-made gifts of handcrafted earrings.

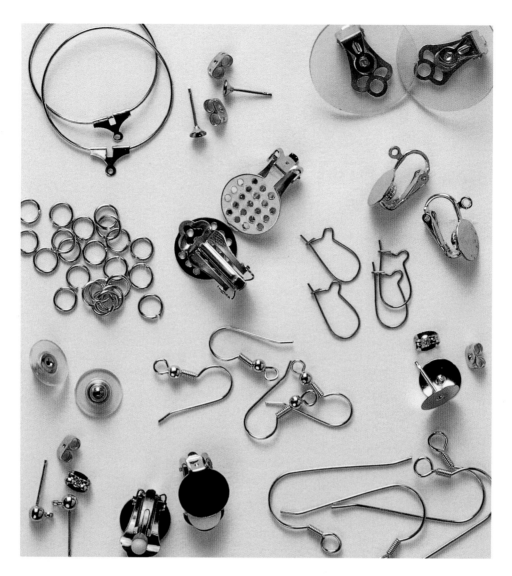

The Real Facts on Findings

EARRING TOOLS
AND MATERIALS

You can create earrings out of almost anything. If you can figure out the mechanics of attaching an object to an ear wire, post, or clip, you can assemble an earring in no time. All you need are a few readily available tools and a knowledge of "findings," the general name for earring hardware.

Because earrings are so small, you shouldn't go broke when investing in supplies. You may already have just what you need tucked away in your supply cabinet or family tool chest. If you need to purchase tools, you can find them at local hardware stores or craft-supply shops. Findings are available at craft and bead shops, or through jewelry-supply catalogs.

BASIC TOOLS

Pliers

If you've ever had to buy a pair of pliers, you know the choices are astounding. Don't let this discourage you. You'll need only three basic pliers for these projects: round-nose, needle-nose, and flat-nose. Since you will most often be using pliers with metal findings, you want smooth-jaw pliers, not serrated-jaw which will mar the metal as you work.

Just remember you'll be working small so you want to buy or use a pair that is more suitable for delicate work than for large engine repair.

Cutters

You will need wire cutters for trimming head pins and snipping lengths of wire. Diagonal cutters have pointed ends and blades on the inside of the jaws. They are perfect for getting into small spaces.

Files

You'll find many uses for a good set of small, fine, hand files. They are essential for removing burrs (those rough edges left after cutting metal), but you'll also use them for smoothing the edges of gourds, or shaping baked polymer clay.

FINDINGS

Whether you have pierced or unpierced ears there's a finding that's right for you and for the project you're making. If you have a known reaction to metals, it's best to use findings that are hypo-allergenic. Most people will not have a problem with findings that are gold or silver.

Wires

French, Spanish, and kidney wires have different names but follow the same basic principle—you insert one end of a thin, curved wire into the pierced lobe while the other end, which has a loop suitable for attaching your earring component, remains on the outside of the lobe.

The wires differ only slightly in the way they stay in the lobe. French wires have a curve and generous length of wire that hangs behind the lobe to help keep the wire from slipping out. Kidney wires have a small loop and hook that you fasten after inserting the wires. Spanish wires go a step further. They have a hinged, grooved catch that you open before inserting the wire, then once the wire is in, you close the catch which holds tight to the wire making the earring very secure.

The wires you choose are a matter of personal preference based on your comfort and on the project you're making. For instance, you'll need a more secure wire or finding when making heavier earrings so they'll hang properly. You may also want more security from a finding when making earrings that use a special memento, bead, stone, or charm that you don't want to risk losing.

Posts

Posts are thin rods of metal that you insert into your lobe and secure at the back with an "ear nut," a piece that slips over the post to prevent the earring from coming out of the lobe.

You use glue to attach a post to the earring. While you can invest in jewelry adhesive, a good, strong, quick-drying glue will work. Just make sure it is suitable for gluing metal. Be careful when you glue. Try to confine the glue to the points of contact. Some people may get allergic reactions to the glue if it touches their skin.

Ear nuts come in many shapes. All you really need to know is that the ear nut should correspond to the thickness of the post. If you are considering making a heavier earring that takes a post, use a clutch nut with a stabilizer disk. Once you get over thinking you've stumbled into a auto-repair shop, you'll understand that a clutch is an ear nut with an internal spring that keeps it snug on the post and a stabilizer disk is a large plastic circle that fits against the back of the lobe. The disk distributes the weight of the earring, while the clutch holds it tight to help prevent any discomfort from sagging earrings that can pull on the lobe.

Jump Rings

A jump ring is a small circle of wire with an opening on its circumference that acts as a connector between the pieces of your earrings. Never overlook this humble finding. It is the flying buttress of jewelry design and can take you to new levels of design. You will use it most often to attach your earring component to the findings or for assembling earrings with multiple parts. A jump ring helps an earring hang properly and serves to give it some movement. You can buy different sizes of ready-made jump rings or make your own.

When using a jump ring, always open and close it sideways. If you pull a jump ring open, you'll weaken the metal and the jump ring will loose its spring, making it more susceptible to opening at the wrong times. (Have you ever been the victim of beads down the bodice or earrings in the soup?) If you need more security from a jump ring, use a split ring; it has a double circle of wire and works like a key ring.

Clips

Some people with unpierced ears claim there's a conspiracy against them. They often tell how it's much easier to find earrings for pierced ears. Learning to make your own earrings can help solve this dilemma. By substituting a clip or screw back finding, you can easily make the earrings in this book.

Clips come in many different styles and sizes. The basic principle is that a hinged, spring mechanism grips the lobe from behind. The front of the clip has either a flat "pad," a surface for attaching the earring component, or a loop for suspending drop or dangle earrings. You will also find clips with perforated pads designed for attaching fabric or beadwork.

Clips can be uncomfortable to wear for long periods of time. Heavier earrings need stronger springs which have a tendency to pull the lobes, causing discomfort. Many devices have been invented to ease this problem. Slip-on cushions that pad the lobe, improved springs and hinges, and ways to adjust the finding's tension now make clip-ons more comfortable to wear.

Screw-back findings have a threaded screw mechanism that holds the earring to the lobe. They are not as strong as clips so are more suitable for lighter-weight designs.

Transforming earrings designed for pierced ears to clips or screw backs is fairly easy. While not all pierced earrings can be converted, there are many findings that can help you make the change. If you can't find what you need at a craft store or through a jewelry-supply catalog, your local jeweler should be able to help you.

BEADS

Beads and earrings—what a perfect match! Beads show their incredible versatility as one of the most favorite earring materials. Whether they're strung on a head pin, wrapped with wire, or worked with needle and thread, beads continue to glisten and gleam on earlobes as they have done for thousands of years. With all the incredible choices available today, you could devote the rest of your life to beading without exhausting potential patterns and color schemes.

DONNA ZALUSKY
Lampworked Glass Leaves

If you've already succumbed to the charm of beads, you know the level of enthusiasm beaders have for their craft. Spend time with other beaders and you'll hear almost poetic discourses on matte delicas, Japanese delicious, lampwork glass, and bugles. Once you learn the vocabulary, you'll find that talking "beads" is a universal language shared throughout the world.

If you are one of the uninitiated—proceed with caution. Once you begin with beads, there's no turning back. Walk into a bead shop and you'll be struck by the incredible colors and variety of beads available to you; wood, stone, metal, glass—beads from all over the world or made by local artisans.

You will lose your heart—and possibly your head—as you go about discovering and selecting your treasures. When you recover, you'll find yourself with way too many tiny bags of beads begging to be made into projects. Now what? Keep your wits about you—start small. And what better way to begin (or continue) your journey with beads than by making earrings.

Know Your Beads

STRINGING

Tools, Materials, and Basics

The basic techniques for stringing beads are rather straightforward, the skill of combining beads into a beautiful design is its art. Many of your inspirations for creating bead earrings will come from the beads themselves. Shape, size, color, finish, or faceting will lead you to create just the right style. Play with the beads. (An encouragement most of you don't need.) Arrange them several times until you get them where you want them. Mix a variety of beads for a harmonious design, or let a special bead stand alone. (For one designer's insight into creating bead earrings, see "Tips From Thalia" on pages 18–19.)

If you are looking for beads to string and have questions about their size, think in millimeters. To give you an indication of some sizes, see Figure 1. Be aware of the weight of the beads you use for earrings. Avoid beads that are too heavy to prevent distended lobes for pierced ears or pulled lobes with clips. Save your heaviest beads for coordinating necklaces.

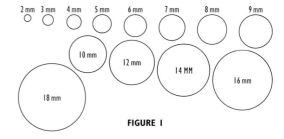

FIGURE I

KATE DREW-WILKINSON
Dramatic Uses for Swarovski Crystals

CAROL PERRENOUD
"Mrs. Frank Lloyd Wright"

ROUND-NOSE PLIERS, FLAT-NOSE PLIERS, AND DIAGONAL WIRE CUTTERS are all the basic tools you'll need (see page 9). Since eye pins, head pins, or wire are the most common materials used for stringing beads for earrings, these tools allow you to cut, bend, and twist the wire as you work.

HEAD PINS AND EYE PINS resemble fat needles. They come in different lengths and are available wherever you can purchase jewelry findings. A head pin has a flat bottom that acts as a stopper for the first bead. An eye pin has a loop on the bottom that also acts as a stopper for the first bead while providing you with a way to attach fringe, charms, or more beads.

When working with eye pins and head pins, you need to remember to leave at least a ¼- to ⅜-inch (.5 cm–1 cm) end at the top for making a loop. If you happen to have more than that when you're finished stringing your beads, clip the excess with wire cutters.

KATE DREW-WILKINSON
*4000-Year-Old Beads
from the Indus Valley*

TO MAKE A LOOP (Figure 2), first clip any excess, then take your round-nose pliers and grasp the end of the wire. Roll the pliers, shaping the wire around the jaw of the pliers. If you need to open this loop, always open it sideways like a jump ring. If you just pull at the loop to open it, you'll weaken the metal, lessening its holding power.

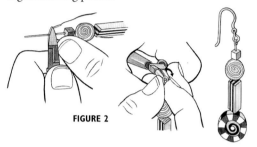

FIGURE 2

WIRE comes in different gauges, an indication of its diameter—the larger the gauge number the thinner the wire. Twenty-gauge, a common size for stringing beads, is thinner than 16-gauge wire which is more suitable for bent wire jewelry. If you decide to string your beads on wire, you can creatively wrap the wire for a decorative effect before making your loop. (Glass-bead artist Kimberley Adams shows on page 20 how to create a bent wire coil with a built-in ear post for stringing a beautiful handmade bead.)

CHAINS, CORD, AND LEATHER are some other materials you can use for stringing your beads. Whatever you choose, you will need to have a loop at the end for attaching the finding. For chain, simply slip in a jump ring through the last link. For cord and leather, you will need to attach a crimp, a metal coil or bead that grips the cord. It will give your project a finished look and provide you with a loop for attaching your finding.

TO USE A CRIMP, slip it over the ends of your cord or leather when you have finished stringing your beads. Then, with your flat-nose pliers, squeeze the bottom coil of the crimp until it firmly grasps the cord.

WEAVING

Tools, Materials, and Basics

Bead weaving includes off-loom and on-loom techniques. The projects in this book are all done with off-loom stitches. To get started, all you need are the beads, a few supplies, and a working knowledge of three basic stitches: the flat peyote stitch, the Comanche or brick stitch, and the flat square stitch.

SEED BEADS are the beads you'll use for your weaving projects. Even if you're not a beader, it's hard to avoid the seduction of seed beads—they're so colorful, so beautiful, and so, so, small. Once you see them you will realize they're aptly named. New beaders will tell you seed beads range in size from barely visible to hardly manageable. But the more you work with them, the more skilled you'll become in handling their size.

Seed beads come in numbered sizes that are written this way: 6° and 11° (a smaller number denotes a larger bead). They come in a variety of shapes: delicas—squared cylinders; bugles—narrow tubes; and round cylinders. And they come in a variety of finishes: matte; glossy; lined; unlined; and metallic. You can find commercially available containers and trays that will help you keep your seed beads organized both for storage and while you're beading.

NEEDLES AND THREAD are the basic tools and material you'll need to work with seed beads. Beading needles come in sizes written like this: #12, #14. For these projects, you'll need the needles that look like regular needles rather than flexible needles that resemble twisted wire. Whether you're beading or sewing, threading a needle can be a challenge. Try to find needles with eyes that are relatively large but can still pass easily through the bead's hole.

BEAD THREAD that is strong, durable, and able to make several passes through a bead with a little extra room to spare, is essential. While earrings don't get heavy wear, you don't want them coming apart. It's rather embarrassing to watch helplessly as hundreds of tiny seed beads dance happily over the floor. Bead weavers prefer the new synthetics. Thread sizes correspond to their thickness and are written as capital letters, as in B and D.

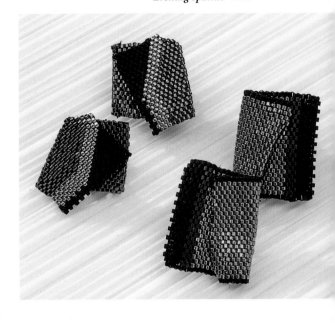

BEAD GLUE, a glue for securing the knots you make in bead thread, will help to keep the knots tied, giving you an extra measure of security for keeping your beadwork together.

BEESWAX, for waxing your thread, gives the thread extra body while your work. Just make a few passes with the thread on the beeswax. Don't apply too much or you will end up with annoying stray flakes of wax or dirty wax balls on your finished beadwork.

STITCHES

These basic directions for the stitches should help you get started. In the individual instructions for the projects, the designers give you the steps for modifying these stitches to fit their designs.

If you've never worked with seed beads and needles before, you may want to spend time getting familiar with the process. For your sample work, begin with the larger-size seed beads—6° works well. If you feel adventurous, use delicas—they are about size 12° with bigger holes that are easy to find.

Flat Peyote Stitch

Peyote stitch is versatile and popular. Once you learn it you can apply it to many different designs. You can work peyote stitch in a tubular pattern or as a flat stitch. Since the projects use flat peyote stitch, begin with these instructions.

1. Thread your needle.

2. String on a bead, leaving a 4-inch (10 cm) tail. Loop around and pass the needle through the bead again to anchor it. (This is sometimes called a stopper bead.)

3. To make your base strand, string on seven more beads (for a total of eight). Pick up another bead as in Figure 3.

FIGURE 3

4. Work right to left as you take your needle back through bead #7. Pick up another bead and take your needle through bead #5. Continue picking up a bead, then entering every other bead, until you have worked the row as in Figure 4. Pick up bead #13.

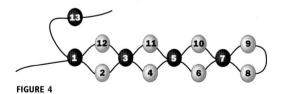

FIGURE 4

5. You want to keep working right to left, so when you finish a row, turn the work around. Bead #13 will be to your right as in Figure 5. Pass the needle through bead #12, and continue as you did in Step 4 until you've completed another row. Continue working this way until you feel comfortable with this pattern.

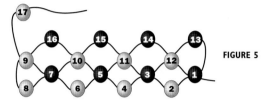

FIGURE 5

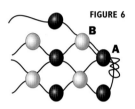

FIGURE 6

TO DECREASE: Exit your last bead and make several loops around the edge thread. Take the needle through bead A, then bead B (or however many you want to decrease). Pick up a bead and work the stitch to the end (see Figure 6).

TO INCREASE: Pick up as many beads as you need for your increase at the end of a row. String on one more bead. This extra bead will become the first bead of the next row. Pass the needle through what is now the next-to-the-last bead of the last row (hint: this is one of the beads you added for the increase). Pick up a bead and continue working the stitch as you did in Step 4.

Comanche Stitch/Brick Stitch

You can usually spot Comanche stitch earrings by their triangular shape and dangling fringe. Because of its resemblance to a brick wall, the Comanche Stitch is also known as the brick stitch. This stitch creates a triangle, with the base row always being the widest. As you work "up," you're naturally decreasing one bead for every row.

Barbara Elbe has included the basics of Comanche stitch in her instructions for her birdhouse earrings (page 28). Follow her diagrams in Steps 4 and 5 to learn how to work this stitch. Then once you feel comfortable with the technique, go on to make the rest of the earrings!

Flat Square Stitch

In flat square stitch you stitch one bead over the other, making the beads line up in neat vertical and horizontal rows. This gives square stitch the look of bead work made on a loom. To work the stitch, you pass the thread through the beads, connecting them in a looping pattern. When you finish a row, and before beginning the next, pass the thread directly through the row above, then pass it directly through the row you just made. Then begin the next row. Because you pass the thread through the rows so many times, square stitch is very strong.

1. Thread your needle. Pass the needle through the first bead and loop around to secure. String on five more beads. To start the next row, string on bead #7 and line it up below bead #6. Pass the needle up through bead #6, making a loop, then pass the needle down through bead #7 as in Figure 7. Add beads by looping through the bead directly above. Continue to square stitch until you get back to bead #1 as in Figure 8.

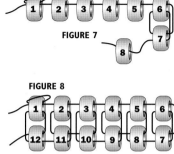

FIGURE 7

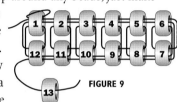

FIGURE 8

2. Following Figure 9, pass the thread all the way through the top row. Do not loop around any beads, just make a direct pass. Then pass the thread through the row you just completed. Once you finish a row you will always make a direct pass through the row above, then another direct pass through the row you just completed.

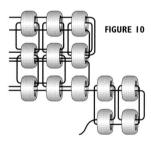

FIGURE 9

TO INCREASE: String on as many beads as you need for your increase as in Figure 10, and begin working the next row as in Step 1. If you are increasing on the other side, you'll need to add beads to fill the gaps (see Figure 11).

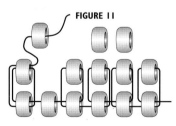

FIGURE 10

FIGURE 11

TO DECREASE: Exit the bead where you want to decrease and continue with your next row (see Figure 12). Make sure to pass directly through the row above, exiting at your decrease.

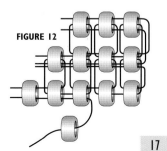

FIGURE 12

MARJI BROHAMMER
Square Stitch Feathers

DESIGNER: *Thalia Tringo*

Tips From Thalia

DESIGN POSSIBILITIES
FOR EXPANDING YOUR
EARRING REPERTOIRE

Thalia Tringo is a lampworker and jewelry designer who works out of her studio in Cambridge, Massachusetts. But she doesn't stop there. She teaches beading and glass beadmaking, is a buyer for a well-known bead shop, is active in her local bead society, and lectures and consults on jewelry and craft marketing.

Thalia's extensive experience with beads prompts her to share her design insights. She hopes that they'll help you organize your own ideas into action and will be the beginning of many wonderful pairs of beaded earrings.

WHEN I WAS SHOWN HOW to make a pair of earrings, I felt like a cavewoman being shown fire for the first time. The process wasn't complicated. I put beads on a head pin, made a loop at the top, connected the loop to an ear wire and there it was—I made an earring. I was inspired.

I bought individual beads, strands of beads, and old jewelry to take apart. I found dozens of styles of ear wires. My supply of head pins would last through several lifetimes of beading. I explored the impact of shape, color, length, and style on design. But after making several dozen pairs, I began to feel constrained by the single head pin format. Although what I made looked great, I began asking myself some basic questions. What if you wanted an earring that moved? How do you assemble a multi-strand necklace? What if you must use an object for your earring and it doesn't have a hole for stringing? All of these questions (and many more!) led me to develop or discover techniques that would solve my design dilemmas.

MULTISTRAND EARRINGS

Multistrand earrings can dazzle the eye with layers of color. They are an excellent match with multistrand necklaces. To make multistrand earrings, you will need to use cones. As their name implies, they are cone-shaped pieces of metal used for covering the knots you make when stringing beads, giving your piece a finished look.

To begin, string beads on several earring-length strands of cord. Leave a tail of 3 inches (7.5 cm) or more of exposed cord at the end of each strand. Stiffen and fortify the exposed cord by rubbing it with beeswax. Tie the group of strands in a square knot around a 2-inch (5 cm) piece of wire or head pin. Seal the knot with bead cement or clear nail polish. Pull the wire through a cone to cover the knot. Use the remaining wire to make a loop. Cut off the excess wire. Attach an ear wire to the loop.

MUSICAL EARRINGS

You've explored the visual impact of color, length, shape, and motion in design, but what about arousing another sense? A small colorful jingle bell suspended from a chain is a lightweight, subtle holiday greeting. Or try using the lovely silver clapper bells that are often featured on anklets from India. If you are a technical wizard, you may find a way to incorporate a computer sound chip similar to the type used in musical greeting cards.

CORD

Leather, genya, hemp, waxed cotton, or other heavy cords can be used to make youthful, rugged earrings featuring metal charms or other heavy components. Satin or other thick fabric cords offer a sleek, contemporary alternative to the rough-hewn look of leather. A heavy black satin cord earring with bright silver or gold components makes a striking simple statement.

To give your cord earrings a finished look, use a crimp bead or coil. To make the shell earrings, start with a piece of leather cord 5/8 inches (1.6 cm) longer than the amount you need for your design. String on the shell. Insert both ends of the cord into the crimp coil. Using flat-nose pliers, squeeze only the last coil of wire on the crimp (the coil that is at the opposite end of the loop). Squeeze the coil until the cord is secure in the crimp. Open the loop on the crimp and attach your ear wire.

COLORFUL EARRINGS

Use materials that capture attention, such as beads with vivid or neon colors, fluorescent plastic findings, anodized aluminum cones, niobium coils, or coated glass beads that reflect light like a prism.

ASYMMETRICAL EARRINGS

Show off your creativity with asymmetrical earrings. You can make different styles based on theme, artistic inspiration, or shape reversals. To make thematic pairs, choose two different but related shapes such as cat and fish, or sun and moon. For artistic pairs, use different related shapes such as a solid circle and a hollow circle, or feature different imagery from a matching necklace or pin. Reversing shapes is another good way to emphasize the impact of shape and design. Simply reverse the order of the beads on each earring—this can completely transform the look.

JOINTED EARRINGS

A jointed, or segmented earring gives movement and flexibility without the rigidity, weight, and length of a long earring on a single head pin. To make jointed earrings start by stringing beads on a head pin, leaving enough room to make a loop at the top. Make a loop, then take a piece of wire and bend it around the loop. Or, take an eye pin and attach the eye to the loop. String beads on the wire/eye pin, making a loop at the top for attaching your ear wire. Make as many segments as you want.

DESIGNER:
Kimberley Adams

Golden Swirls

If you can't figure out a great way to set a special bead, follow these instructions for creating a simple and elegant coil. You'll be making your own ear posts so be sure to use silver, gold, or gold-filled wire.

MATERIALS

- 20- and 22-gauge sterling, gold, or gold-filled wire
- Small beads, size 6°, 8°, or 10°
- 2 larger "focus" beads (special beads you wish to highlight)
- 2 ear nuts

TOOLS

- Round-nose pliers
- Flat-nose pliers
- Wire cutters

INSTRUCTIONS

1. Begin by making the top spiral that will become the ear post. Cut a 4-inch (10 cm) length of wire.

2. Using the flat-nose pliers, bend the wire to make a right angle about ⅝ inch (1.6 cm) from one end.

3. Grasp the right angle in the pliers. Hold just enough of the long end of wire, approximately ⅟₁₆ inch (.16 cm), and bend the wire around the side of the pliers. You should have something like a C, which is perpendicular to the ⅝-inch (1.6 cm) section (see Figure 1.)

4. Pinch that "C" very close to the end of the pliers. The long end of wire should extend from the side of the pliers.

5. Begin bending that wire around the "C" to make the spiral as in Figure 2, moving the spiral in a circular motion as you work. Keep the wire extending toward the end of the pliers —not down toward your hand.

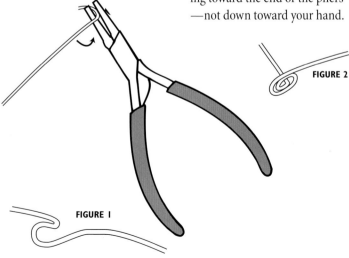

FIGURE 2

FIGURE 1

6. Continue bending the wire until you have the size spiral you need. Leave a straight end extending from the end of the spiral that is at least ⅝ inch (1.6 cm) long. You will use this to make a "leg" for stringing the small beads and making the end loop.

7. To do this, hold the straight end coming off the spiral and bend it at a right angle in relation to the spiral as in Figure 3.

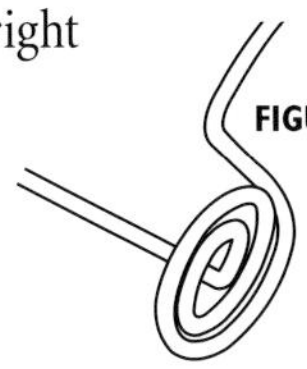

FIGURE 3

8. Hold the spiral and wrap the small section left between the right angle and the spiral onto the spiral as in Figure 4. If necessary, trim the end of the wire to ⅝ inch (1.6 cm).

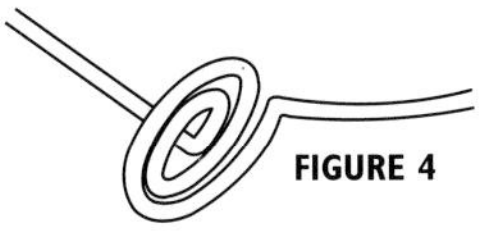

FIGURE 4

9. Thread the size 6° and 8° beads on the wire. Using the round-nose pliers, make a loop.

10. To make the drop, cut a 4-inch (10 cm) length of 22-gauge wire.

11. Use the flat-nose pliers to hold one end of the wire ¹⁄₁₆ inch (.16 cm) from the end. Follow Step 5, coiling the wire around itself to make a small spiral as in Figure 5.

FIGURE 5

12. Make a right angle as in Step 7.

13. Drop on a great bead and a few smalls. (It's up to you!)

14. To make a closed loop, use the round-nose pliers to grab the wire just above the top bead. Wrap the wire around one of the jaws of the pliers.

15. Use the flat-nose pliers to bend the wire around the section of wire going into the bead as in Figure 6.

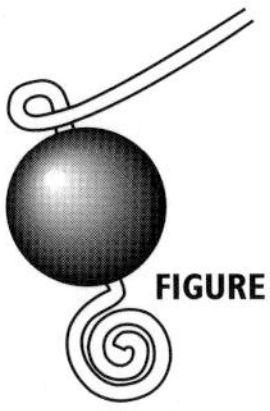

FIGURE 6

16. Wrap the wire completely around the wire going into the bead, then cut the wire close to the wrapping and use the flat-nose pliers to push any end flush to the wrapping.

17. Open the loop at the bottom of the post section and attach the drop to that loop. Remember to open and close any loop sideways; never pull it open.

18. Use ear nuts to fit the posts.

TIPS

• *Since you are creating your own ear posts, you need to use silver, gold, or gold-filled wire to prevent any allergic reactions. While you're learning to make the coils, first practice on copper, brass, or base-metal wire since they are less expensive than silver or gold.*

• *If you find that you are getting dents or crimps in your wire, use tape to wrap the jaws of the pliers.*

prescription earrings

It is believed that the use of metallic ear ornaments began in Asia. This may be distantly related to the ancient Chinese practice of acupuncture where sharp needles are inserted into the skin at various points through-out the body to stimulate healing and promote good health. In acupuncture, certain points in the ear are said to relate to the cure of deafness and to help poor eyesight.

Piercing a child's ears to prevent diseases of the eye and ear was a preva-lent practice throughout Europe for many cen-turies. In America this practice continued into the early part of this century, due in part to the large influx of immi-grants from all over the world.

DESIGNER: *Melanie Alter*

Simply Charming

In a few short steps, you can create beautiful designs from wire, beads, ready-made charms, buttons, and pendants. Select your jewelry components, add a creative touch, and you'll have earrings that make a personal statement.

Black-Bronze Dangle Earrings

MATERIALS

- 22-gauge round, red brass wire— red brass has more copper than zinc in it, giving the brass a reddish color
- Beads and charms
- 2 jewelry components with multiple loops for suspending dangles
- Earring posts or ear wires
- Strong glue or solder

TOOLS

- Round-nose pliers
- Wire cutters

INSTRUCTIONS

1. Determine how long you want your dangles. Add 1½ inch (4 cm) to that length for wrapping the wire. According to that measurement, cut as many pieces of wire as you'll need.

2. At one end of the wire, make a loop for holding the charms and attach.

3. String the beads on the wire.

4. Thread the wire through one of the loops of the jewelry component with multiple loops.

5. Bend the wire to make a loop, then wrap the excess wire around the top of the wire to finish. In order to wrap the wire evenly, hold the round-nose pliers in your right hand (or left), and prop your other arm against your work table for support.

6. Attach an ear wire through the top loop of the component with multiple loops, or glue or solder a post or clip to the back. If soldering, use silver solder.

VARIATIONS

Bone-Silver Drop Earrings

Follow the same procedures for the black-bronze dangles. To create the top portion of the earring, thread wire through the top of the jewelry component with multiple loops and through a glass ring. Wrap the excess wire to finish. Glue a round silver charm or decorative button over the hole in the glass ring. Glue or solder a post or clip.

Pendant & Button

Thread the wire through the dangle charm and make a loop. Thread on the bead. Then bring the wire through the button shank and wrap the wire behind the button. Glue or solder a post or clip.

DESIGNER:
Carol Perrenoud

Kinky Fringe

*Designer Carol Perrenoud uses the kinky
fringe described in her business partner's
book, Virginia Blakelock's "Those Bad Bad
Beads," to create these earrings. Carol says,
"Even though they look very modern,
wild, and eclectic, we have seen pictures
of ready-made beaded Victorian trim
that is also kinky fringe."*

*Don't hold back—just a few fringe can
look skimpy. The more fringe you make,
the more wonderful and alive it looks.*

MATERIALS

- Size 11° seed beads, one to
  several colors
- Bead thread, size D in a color
  to match or complement beads
- Bead glue or clear nail polish
- Ear posts
- Scrap of sueded fabric that
  matches the bead color
- Small piece of medium-weight
  plastic (plastic from a milk jug
  works well)

TOOLS

- Scissors
- 2 beading needles, #12
- Thin piercing tool

INSTRUCTIONS

1. Work in a place with good
lighting. Cut a length of thread
2 yards (1.8 m) long. Using two
needles, thread a needle on each
end of the thread.

2. Make a seed bead ladder.
Using one of the needles, string
one seed bead and let it glide to
the center of the thread. Pick up
a second bead and leave it on the
needle. Take the second needle
and go through this bead in the
opposite direction from the first
needle. The needles will be
crossed through the bead. (See
Figures 1A and 1B.)

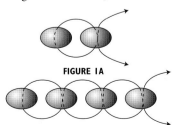

FIGURE 1A

3. Pull the needles in opposite
directions until the second bead
is snug up against the first bead.
Continue making the ladder by
picking up one bead at a time,
crossing the needles through it,
then pulling up the thread in
opposite directions. Make the
ladder 7 to 11 beads long. This
is the base of the woven diamond so the longer it is, the
wider and larger the diamond.

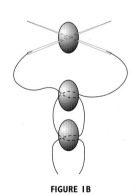

FIGURE 1B

4. At the end of the ladder, make a locking stitch similar to a backstitch. Take one needle and retrace the thread path through the previous bead, then back through the last bead so you end up where you started. The thread should make a back-wards circle (see Figure 2). *Note:* From now on you will be using only one needle at a time so remove the needle that you are not currently using, letting the end of the thread dangle.

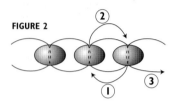

FIGURE 2

5. The base of the diamond is worked in Comanche stitch or brick stitch. To start, pick up one bead and stitch under the thread between the beads of the previous row. (The point of the needle should be coming toward you.) Pull the thread all the way up and snug, then go back through the bead that you just picked up so that the point of the needle is now going away from you (see Figure 3).

6. Two of the stitching motions will secure each bead so make two passes of the thread through each bead. At the end of every other row, the thread shows on the outside of the bead. (Don't worry, that's why you have matching thread.) Each row will automatically decrease one bead. Continue working until there is only one bead in the row. *Note:* Try flipping the piece over at the end of every row. You may find that working with the rows progressing towards your body makes the stitching motion feel more natural and comfortable for your wrist.

7. Pull the needle off this thread and thread the needle with the other end of the thread you've left dangling. Make another woven triangle on the back side of the seed bead ladder. When you are done with the base, you will have a diamond shape.

8. Using the needle and thread, weave diagonally through the beads on the edge until you reach the end of the ladder row (see Figure 4).

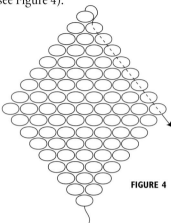

FIGURE 4

9. Now the fringes begin! Think of the trunk of a tree with branches. String all the beads for the trunk first. Slide the last bead you've strung out of the way and go back through a few beads and emerge from the trunk with the needle. Grasp the last "terminal" bead with your fingertips and pull tightly on the thread with your other hand.

10. Now make a "branch" as in Figure 5 by stringing a few beads, go around the last bead you strung (the terminal bead) and go back through the other beads of the branch. Pull tightly again by grasping the termi-

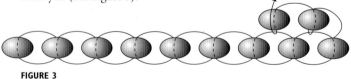

FIGURE 3

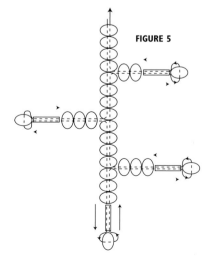

FIGURE 5

nal bead and pulling on the thread. Tighten the tension of each branch separately before re-entering the trunk and emerging to make another branch. *(The right tension on these fringes is crucial to their success.)* The tighter the tension of the thread, the more the side branches of the fringe will stick out and hold their shape. If the tension loosens up, the side branches tend to sag and droop and can now be referred to as "feather" fringe.

11. Make more branches until you reach the base. Enter the next bead on the edge of the woven base from the top and come out the bottom. The fringe actually hangs between the beads of the base (Figure 6). You can make the fringes longer as you progress toward the tip of the base.

FIGURE 6

12. Tie off the thread when you have 6 inches (15 cm) of thread left. With the threaded needle, go through two beads in the base. Dip under the threads between two beads and pull it up till there is a small loop of thread remaining. Go back through that loop with the needle and pull tightly. This is just like making a regular sewing knot.

13. Seal the knot with a dab of bead glue or clear nail polish. Go through a few more beads and tie another knot. Seal the knot, go through a few more beads to bury the tail, then cut the thread. Pick up the other length of thread that was left over from making the original ladder and continue to make fringes with it. *Note:* If your thread breaks and you need to add a length of thread, reverse the sequence of events for tying off a thread. Go through a few beads, tie a knot, go through a few more beads, tie another knot, then go through the beads necessary to come out where you need to continue working. If your thread tends to break or tangles easily, you may want to wax it *lightly*. If you wax it too heavily, dirty wax balls will form between the beads.

14. Trace around the diamond base onto your scrap of ultra suede. Cut the fabric just inside the drawn line on the fabric. Cut a tiny hole in the center for the ear post.

15. From the plastic, cut a diamond, one bead-width small, all the way around. Use a sharp tool to pierce a hole in the plastic diamond's center. First, push the post through the plastic, then the fabric. (The plastic acts as a stabilizer between the beads and fabric.)

16. Whipstitch the fabric all the way around the base of the earring by stitching between the beads and around the thread. When done, tie a knot and bury the tail. Make your other earring to match or to drastically *not* match for an asymmetrical look.

TIPS

• *Use lighter beads on the tips of the fringes to create an optical illusion that makes the fringes appear fuller and more three dimensional.*

• *If you use bugle beads in the side branches, buffer them on each side with a seed bead. The thread is less likely to shred and break against the sharp edges of the bugle beads.*

• *Don't always use the same number of beads for the side branches. Vary the lengths, just like a tree, with shorter branches at the tip and longer branches near the woven base of the earring.*

DESIGNER:
Fran Stone

Peyote Stitch on a Pi Ring

Add basic flat peyote stitch to the simple shape of a Chinese Pi ring, and you have earrings that are elegant and easy-to-make.

MATERIALS

- 2 Pi circles, 1 inch (2.5 cm) in diameter
- 2 grams of Japanese cylinder beads—two or three colors, depending on your design

TOOLS

- Beading needle, #12
- Multifilament thread, size B
- Ear wires

INSTRUCTIONS

TECHNIQUE: *Flat Peyote Stitch, page 16*

1. Thread the #12 needle with 1 yard (.9 m) of size B thread.

2. Put 10 beads on a single thread. (If the Pi is larger than 1 inch (2.5 cm), add additional beads to accommodate the width of the Pi ring.)

3. Using the flat peyote stitch, create a geometric design (or whatever you wish!). Just remember to use an odd number of beads if you create a design that requires a center. Using an even number of beads is easier and faster to work.

4. Complete enough rows to equal the diameter of the Pi ring. (A one-inch (2.5 cm) Pi ring equals one inch (2.5 cm) of beadwork.) You want to bead enough rows so that when you fold the length of beading in half and place the fold on the top of the Pi, half the length will reach to the top of the hole in front and the other half will reach to the top of the hole in the back.

5. On one end, just before you reach the desired length, decrease each side, leaving two beads in the center which you will continue to work. This

"tab" of two-bead rows will become the piece that encircles the hole and connects the back to the front. Make as many of these two-bead rows as you need; this will correspond to the depth of the Pi.

6. When you have made enough two-bead rows and are ready to connect the back to the front, secure the thread by going in and out of the work. Do not cut the thread away.

7. Bring the needle up to the end bead of the last two-bead row. Pass this tab through the hole in the Pi to connect the back to the front. Make sure that the beads alternate from side to side. If they don't, add another row.

8. Join the back and front by passing the needle through alternate sides as in Figure 1. Instead of adding a bead as you do when working the peyote stitch, you are basically using the bead from the opposite side as the filler. Think of it as a zipper closing; as a result, the seam will be invisible.

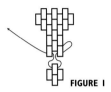

FIGURE 1

9. Secure the thread by going in and out of the work, then cut the thread. Don't worry if the beadwork is too loose for the Pi. You can dab a bit of cement on the inside of the hole to keep the beadwork in place.

10. Now you are ready to add to the top length and make a loop for the ear wire. Begin by working a thread in at the top edge. It will be easy to run a row of beads by working the peyote stitch off this top edge and adding a bead as you did when you set up the first row (see Figure 2).

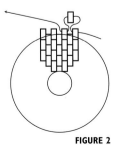

FIGURE 2

11. Work one or two rows, even more if desired, depending on the length you want to achieve. Focus on the two center beads and come out the side of the last bead of this group.

12. Thread eight beads, then come through the outside of the bead on the opposite end of the two-bead group. This will form the loop at the top as shown in Figure 3.

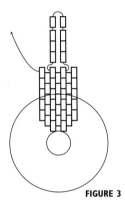

FIGURE 3

13. Work the needle through the beads, positioning it to go through the loop a second time in order to reinforce the work. This loop will hold the ear wire.

14. Secure the thread by zigzagging through the beads before cutting the thread.

15. Make a matching mate and attach the ear wires.

DESIGNER:
Barbara Elbe

Beaded Birdhouse

The typical triangular shape of the Comanche stitch, also known as the brick-laying stitch, creates the perfect slope for the roof line of these beautiful, beaded birdhouses.

MATERIALS

- Delica seed beads, size 11°, in these colors:
  - lined flesh
  - lined magenta
  - silver-lined light green
  - lined sky blue (shimmer)
  - opaque black
  - matte transparent dark topaz
  - matte transparent chocolate brown
- 30, 2mm gold-filled beads
- 8, 4mm amethyst-colored Austrian crystal
- 8, 8mm rectangular bead
- 6, 4mm blue Austrian crystal
- Multifilament thread, size 0
- Beeswax
- 2 ear wires

TOOLS

- Scissors
- Beading needle, #12

INSTRUCTIONS

Note: If you've never worked Comanche stitch, follow Steps 4 and 5 for a basic introduction.

1. Cut a 2-yard (1.8 m) piece of thread. Run the thread across the beeswax two or three times.

2. Thread the needle, positioning the needle so it is approximately 3 inches (7.5 cm) from the end of the thread.

3. Working left to right, pick up the first two beads at the beginning of the base row. Position them half-way on the thread (approximately 36 inches (91.5 cm) from the end). This will allow enough thread for the top half of the earring and enough for the lower section and fringe.

4. Create the base row (15 beads) using this technique:

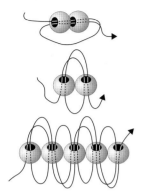

When you get to the end of the row, turn your work.

5. Figure 1 shows the regular beginning of a new row of Comanche or brick stitch. All rows not marked with a number on the chart begin this way. Continue across as shown.

FIGURE I   (1)

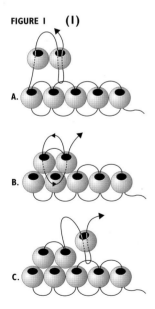

A.

B.

C.

6. The numbers in parentheses next to the rows in the chart correspond to the following instructions and illustrations. Follow these directions as noted in the chart for creating this "uneven" roof line:

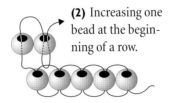

(2) Increasing one bead at the beginning of a row.

(3) Repositioning for a new row that is inset.

(4) Increasing one bead at the end of a row.

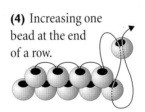

(5) Increasing one bead at the end of a row and starting next row inset by one bead.

7. Work to the top of the pattern. Add trim beads and ear wire.

8. To reinforce: first work the thread back down into the top row of the bead work; then work up the neighboring bead; next, work the thread up through the trim beads; then back down through the trim beads; finish by working back into the bead work.

9. Using a regular sewing knot, tie off on one of the exposed loops between the beads on a lower section of the design. Weave the tail of the thread into the earring and cut.

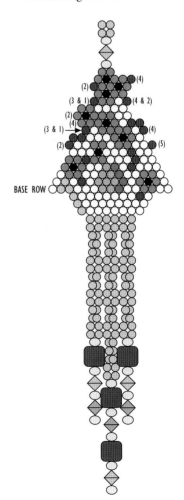

TO MAKE A TWIST FRINGE

1. String the beads for the fringe as shown in the chart for the birdhouse, following the technique illustrated in Figure 2A.

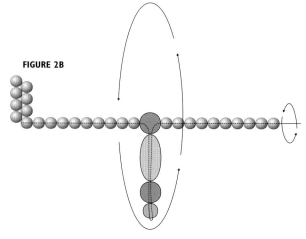

FIGURE 2A

2. After all the beads are in place, stretch the strand out horizontally as in Figure 2B.

3. Twist the thread between the finger and thumb about two or three times up close to the last bead.

4. Hold these twists in place and run the twists off the other end of the thread, letting the needle dangle and twirl in the air. The section with the trim beads should twirl some, distributing the twists. Only the section of thread with beads should have twists, not the empty section of thread in the needle.

FIGURE 2B

5. Repeat this approximately two or three times. While still holding all the twists in place, run the needle up through the bead over to the right along the bottom.

6. Pull the fringe into place, adjusting twists. Go down the next bead to the right with the needle. Repeat across the bottom. Tie off as explained in Step 9 of the earring directions.

DESIGNER:
Fran Stone

Pom-poms

The bouncy fringe on these simple peyote stitch earrings will give you something to cheer about. This versatile design looks as good with casual clothes as it does with dressier outfits.

MATERIALS

- 20- and 22-gauge sterling or gold-filled wire
- Multifilament thread, size B
- 672 round seed beads, size 11°, in color of choice
- 112 round seed beads, size 11°, in contrasting color
- 2 grams of Japanese cylinder beads
- Hollow rod, approximately ¼ inch (.5 cm) in diameter and ¾ inch (2 cm) in length
- 4 glass rondels about ¼ inch (.5 cm) in diameter
- 2 head pins
- Ear wires

TOOLS

- Beading needle, #12
- Needle-nose pliers
- Wire cutters

INSTRUCTIONS

1. Thread approximately 1½ yards (1.4 m) of thread. Do not double the thread; it must be single in order to go through the beads comfortably a number of times.

2. Place eight 11° seed beads on the thread, leaving a 3-inch (7.5 cm) tail as in Figure 1A.

FIGURE 1A

3. To form a ring, bring the needle back to the first bead and go through the eight beads again, drawing them closed.

4. To secure the ring, use a square knot to tie the tail that was left in Step 2 to the basic thread as in Figure 1B.

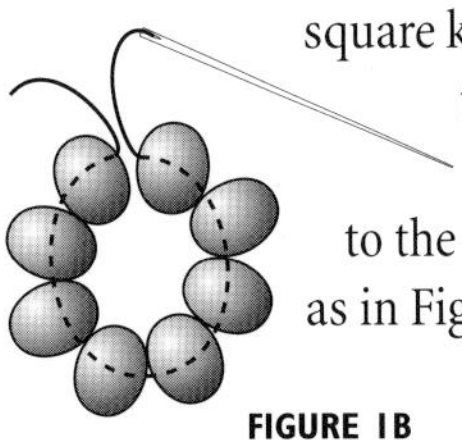

FIGURE 1B

5. On the needle, thread four 11° round beads that are the same color as the ring you just made. Then thread one 11° bead in a contrasting color, then one 11° bead in the same color as the ring.

6. Thread back through the beads, starting with the contrasting bead. The last bead at the tip will be the anchor as in Figure 1C. (This is similar to the standard technique for making fringe.)

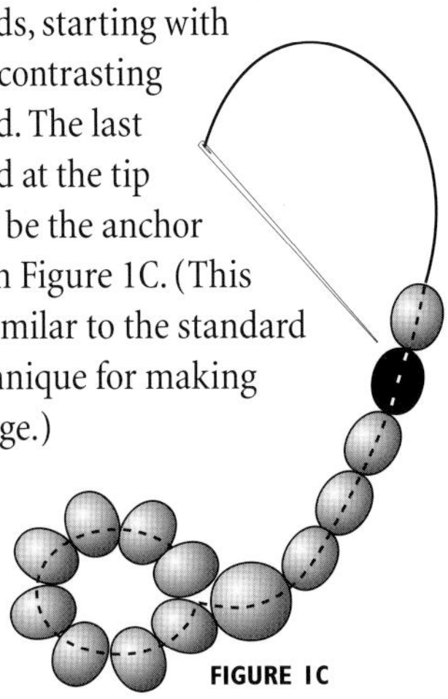

FIGURE 1C

7. Bring the beads down to the ring, eliminating any space between the spike and the ring. Place the needle in the bead next to where the string of beads lay. This will bring you to the right. (See Figure 1D.)

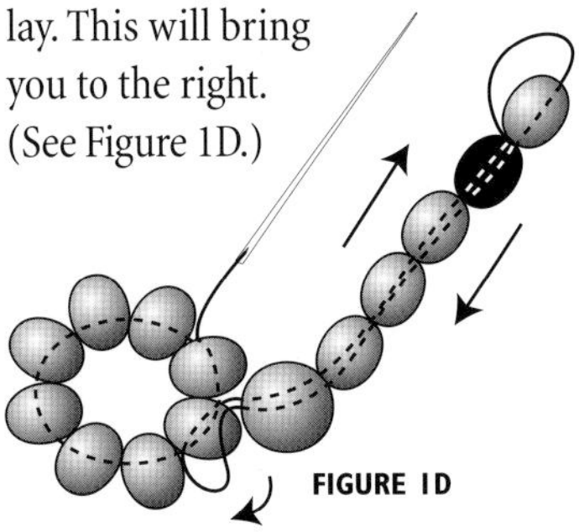

FIGURE 1D

8. Go through this bead and through the bead on the left of the string of beads. This will bring the needle up between the next two beads. In effect, it will be centering the string of beads on top of a bead.

9. Proceed in this fashion until you have eight spikes, each one standing out from the center of a bead on the ring. Secure the thread by going through the ring twice. Cut the thread.

10. Repeat until you make 12 rings with spikes (six for each earring). Put these aside.

11. Thread a needle singly with approximately 1 yard (.9 m) of thread. Put enough 11° Japanese cylinder beads on the needle to accommodate the length of the hollow cylinder.

12. Using the flat peyote technique (page 16), continue until you have enough lines to fit snugly around the diameter of the hollow cylinder.

13. Connect the first line of peyote to the last line. Make sure the beads will fit into each other as in Figure 2.

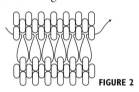

FIGURE 2

14. Cover two of the cylinders in this way.

15. Thread the components in the following sequence on the head pin:

1, ¼-inch (.5 cm) rondel
6 rings with spikes
1 peyote-covered cylinder
1, ¼-inch (.5 cm) rondel

16. Make a loop at the top by first folding the head pin at a right angle. Then cut away the head pin, leaving a little less than ¼ inch (.5 cm). Using the round-nose pliers, create a half loop. Do not close this loop completely until you have inserted the ear wire.

17. Insert the ear wire. Using the needle-nose pliers, bring the end of the head pin to join the other side at the top of the rondel.

DESIGNER:
Linda Chapman

Catch the Wind

Capture the breezy feel of perfect kite weather whenever you wear these high-flying kite and wind sock earrings. The down-to-earth directions for using flat peyote stitch will lift your mood.

MATERIALS

- Bonded nylon 3-ply thread
- Beeswax
- Delica beads in your choice of colors
- Bead glue
- 2 sterling silver jump rings
- 2 Shepherd's hook ear wires

TOOLS

- Peyote stitch graph paper and colored pencils
- Beading needle, #12

INSTRUCTIONS

Wind Sock

TECHNIQUE: *Flat Peyote Stitch, page 16*

1. Design a color scheme using the graph paper and colored pencils.

2. Wax a 2½-yard (2.2 m) piece of thread. Thread on the needle, leaving a 12-inch (30.5 cm) tail.

3. Thread the beads. For the blue and green wind sock, the threading pattern was: 2 blue, 4 green, 2 blue, 4 green, 2 blue, 4 green, 2 blue—20 beads in all. Follow the graph until you have six blue stripes.

4. At this point, your tail and working thread will be at opposite corners of the beadwork.

5. With the working thread, sew the seam closed. The beads should butt into each other. Weave back down to the bottom with the working thread, making sure you come out of a bottom bead. This will be the beginning of your fringe.

6. String 30–36 beads the same color as the bead your needle just exited. Go around the end bead and backstitch twice on the way back up the fringe. Go into the bottom bead of the windsock.

7. Go down through the adjacent bead, repeating the fringe process as in Step 6. Continue this until you have fringe all the way around. If you use a random number of beads (between 30 and 36) you'll get a random feel of wind in the "ribbons."

8. To make the hanger once you've finished the fringe, go to the 12-inch (30.5 cm) tail. Take out the backstitch and thread on 15 beads. Weave down into the body of the wind sock and come back through the hanger at the top. Weave down into the body again and go through the hanger a third time. Weave the remaining tail into the body and trim. Because the delica beads have such big holes, you should have no problem making three passes which will add strength to the beadwork.

Kite

1. Design your color scheme using the peyote stitch graph paper and colored pencils.

2. Wax a 2½-yard (2.2 m) piece of thread. Thread on the needle, leaving a 12-inch (30.5 cm) tail.

3. Thread on 22 purple (or color of your choice) beads, backstitching around the first bead.

4. Work back down with the purple, decreasing at the end of this row.

5. Begin with the red and work the rows, decreasing at the end of each row. The thread will show around the end bead on alternate ends of the row. However, if you use a matching thread (in this case red), it disappears. (I sprinkled in a few orange beads at random—they catch the light and look like sunlight.)

6. Repeat the decreasing rows with red on the other side of the purple center stripe, until one bead remains.

7. Weave the thread to the opposite end of the tail.

8. To make the tail, come out one of the two purple beads. Add on a purple bead, spacing it down the thread about ¼ inch (.5 cm) and backstitch.

9. Repeat until there are six beads on the thread. Leave ½ inch (1.5 cm) of thread after the last bead, then cut the thread. Put a drop of glue on each backstitch for stability.

10. Make a second kite following the steps above but with these differences: use 16 beads for the center (purple) row; and make the tail using 5 beads spaced on the thread. (Remember to put glue on the backstitch.)

11. Using the 12-inch (30.5 cm) starting thread, sew the small kite to the large one, weaving through the beads on both levels so no thread shows. Weave the end into the beadwork and cut.

12. To make the loop for attaching the ear wires, take the 12-inch (30.5 cm) tail on the large kite and thread on 15 purple beads. Go into the end bead on the small kite, weave down a few beads, and come back through the 15 beads. Repeat on the other side, then come back and bury the thread in the small kite. Trim the end. For extra stability, put a touch of glue between the two kites as well.

13. Fasten a jump ring on the loop and attach the ear wire.

DESIGNER:
Melanie Alter

Double-Dangle Pink Pearls

Repetition doesn't have to be boring. These dramatic earrings demonstrate that simple can be stunning by using a single color and style of bead. (And length to the maximum!) They're an example of how easy it is make an incredible pair of earrings when you begin with a good, basic design.

MATERIALS

- 22-gauge round sterling silver wire
- Charms
- Beads
- Triangular jewelry component with multiple holes

TOOLS

- Wire cutters
- Round-nose pliers

INSTRUCTIONS

1. Determine how long you want your dangles. Cut as many pieces of wire to this length as you will need. To give these earrings movement, the dangles are made in two parts. They are attached by loops you make to create one long "jointed" dangle.

2. Attach charms to one end of a piece of wire. This will be the end of the bottom segment. String on the beads. Using the round-nose pliers, make a loop at the top.

3. Take another length of wire and make a loop. String on the beads and make a loop at the top. Attach the two sections at their loops. At this point, you should have one long dangle with a charm on the end that is jointed in the middle with a loop at the top. Make as many dangles as you need.

4. Attach the top loop to the triangular jewelry finding.

5. Attach the ear wire to the top hole of the triangular component.

DESIGNER:
Donna Zalusky

Show Stoppers

Designer Donna Zalusky, a noted lampworker, has made many incredible handmade glass beads. She shares these earrings to demonstrate "a simple construction to show off exciting beads."

MATERIALS

- Two "exciting" beads
- Filler beads to complement
- 2 head pins
- Ear wires

TOOLS

- Round-nose pliers
- Wire cutters

INSTRUCTIONS

1. Choose special beads and filler beads to complement them.

2. Thread the beads onto the head pin in a pleasing order. You may find yourself rearranging them several times until you get a design you like.

3. With the wire cutters, cut the head pin ³/₈ inch (1 cm) longer than the bead arrangement.

4. Use the round-nose pliers to make a loop in the eye of the head pin.

5. Insert the loop of the ear wire into the loop you just made in the eye pin and close. Tip: You may find that using a Spanish ear wire will work better than a fishhook wire. The Spanish wire has a hinged, grooved latch that secures the end of the wire, preventing the wire from slipping out of the ear.

lampwork

Beads made from molten glass that is shaped on a rod are known as lampwork beads. While today's lampworkers use sophisticated torches fueled by propane or natural gas to melt their glass, early lampworkers used the flame of a lamp. While the name may no longer relate to the tools glass artists use today, the term "lampwork" remains as a way to define the process.

To make a glass bead in this way, a lampworker takes a rod of colored glass and heats it with a torch, melting the tip of the rod until it is the consistency of thick honey. Then the artisan winds the molten glass around a "mandrel," a rod that shapes the bead. The mandrel has been coated with a "separator," a preparation that prevents the glass from fusing to the rod, making it easy to remove the bead from the mandrel once the bead has been slow cooled.

A plain bead can be embellished by fusing more colored molten glass to its surface to make raised dots, curving lines, and decorative bands. These design elements are one of the distinguishing marks of lampwork beads.

DESIGNER:
Marji Brohammer

Asymmetrical Rhomboids

The shape may be asymmetrical but the earrings are a perfect match. Because square stitch creates a beaded fabric with a nap, the trick with this design is to reverse the shape through increasing and decreasing so the nap will run "down" on both the left and right sides. Follow the chart on page 37 to help you make the special increases and decreases for this project.

MATERIALS

- 2 yards (1.8 m) beading thread, size B
- Seed beads, size 11° in six colors of your choice

TOOLS

- Beading needle
- Scissors

INSTRUCTIONS

TECHNIQUE: *Square Stitch, page 17*

Right Earring

1. Tie on a "stopper" bead 8–10 inches (20.5–25.5 cm) from the end of the beginning tail.

2. With the bead and tail to the left, string on 14 more beads, as in Figure 1, using your chosen color sequence.

3. Working right to left, square stitch bead 15 to bead 12, following the diagram until the square stitch is made over bead 1. Pick up two edge beads, increasing at the end of the row (see Figure 2). Bring the needle out through one bead only, exiting between the pattern bead and the edge bead.

4. String on the edge bead and the first bead of the pattern, decreasing at the beginning of the row (see Figure 2). Continue square stitching across to the last bead of row two. Pick up a pattern bead and an edge bead and increase.

5. String on an edge bead and the first and second beads of row 4 to increase. Continue across the row to the end where you will be one bead "short." String on an edge bead, securing it by decreasing. (You should come out between the edge bead and the last color bead of row four.)

6. String on an edge bead and the first bead of row five to decrease. Work across the row, ending at the last square-stitched bead in row four. Pick up a pattern bead and edge bead and increase.

7. String on an edge bead and the first two beads of row six to increase. Work across the row, then string on an edge bead, securing with a decrease. The thread should come out between the edge bead and the last bead of row six.

8. Put on a "turn" bead and the first bead of row seven to decrease. Continue square stitching across the row. Pick up two pattern beads and increase. You should end with the tail coming out of row seven. Set aside.

FIGURE I

ENDING TAIL

7
6
5
4
3
2
1

15 14

1 2 3 4 5 6 7 8 9 10 11 12 13

BEGINNING TAIL
(STOPPER BEAD)

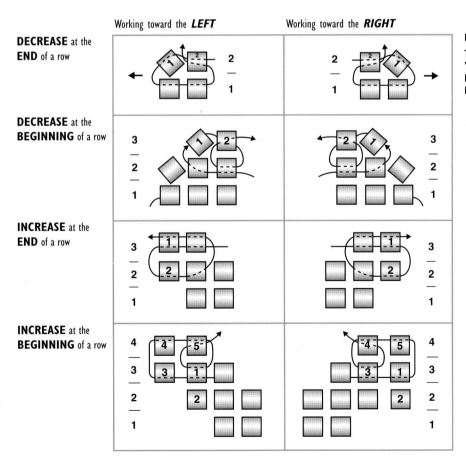

Working toward the **LEFT** Working toward the **RIGHT**

FIGURE 2

THIS CHART WILL HELP YOU MAKE THE SPECIAL INCREASE AND DECREASE FOR THIS PROJECT

DECREASE at the **END** of a row

DECREASE at the **BEGINNING** of a row

INCREASE at the **END** of a row

INCREASE at the **BEGINNING** of a row

Left Earring

1. Tie on a stopper bead as you did for the right earring. Then working with the bead and tail to the left, string on 14 more beads, as in Figure 3.

2. Working right to left, square stitch bead 15 to bead 12. Square stitch across the row until you complete the square stitch over bead 1. Pick up two edge beads, increasing at the end of the row as in Figure 2.

3. String on an edge bead and the first two beads of row three to increase. Work left to right across the row to the end where you will be one bead "short." Put on an edge bead and secure with a decrease.

4. String on an edge bead and the first bead of row four. Decrease, then continue the row to the end. Pick up an edge bead and pattern bead to increase.

5. String on an edge bead and the first two beads of row five, making an increase. Work left to right across to the end of the row (where you will be one bead short). String on the edge bead and secure with a decrease.

6. String on an edge bead and the first bead of row six to decrease. Then continue across the row to the end, picking up a pattern bead and edge bead to make an increase.

7. String on an edge bead and the first two beads of row seven, making an increase. Work left to right across the row, ending with the last square stitch over the last pattern bead. Set aside.

8. To finish, use the end tails to finish the short edge without the hangers first, then put a bead between each edge bead. Knot and hide the end in the beading. Do this for both earrings

9. For the hanger, begin by first untying, then removing the stopper bead. Using the tail, pass the needle through two beads at the end next to the tail (refer to Figures 1 and 3). String on six more beads (five if the beads are "tall") and make a circle of eight beads (or seven).

10. Make several passes through the circle for strength and secure the thread with a knot next to the two beads that are next to the bead work. Continue with the tail up the short side, inserting beads between the edge beads as shown. Secure with a knot and hide it the in the beading. Do this for both earring

FIGURE 3

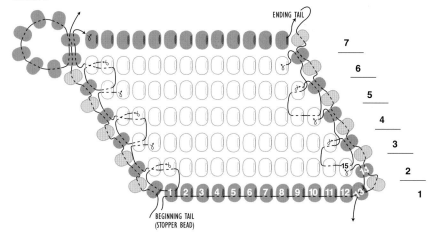

P O L Y M E R
C L A Y

Polymer clay has been on the market for only 30 years, making it one of the newest craft materials. Its popularity continues to spread as artisans discover the incredible potential of this easy-to-use sculpting medium.

POLYMER CLAY is made from polyvinyl chloride (PVC), with added plasticizer to increase its flexibility, and pigments for color. The properties of this clay are what make it a perfect medium for making great earrings: it comes in brilliant colors that are mixable; you bake it in a conventional oven at low temperatures to harden it; it doesn't shrink in the oven; when baked, it is durable and lightweight; and it's nontoxic when used as directed.

You can find polymer in craft shops and through art- and craft-supply catalogs. It comes in small blocks and is produced in a rainbow of colors as well as translucent and pearlized mixtures. In addition, each manufacturer has a line of products that can help you as you work with clay, such as special glues, gloss mediums, thinners, and metallic powders.

The National Polymer Clay Guild, which acts as a nonprofit educational organization, unites thousands of polymer-clay artists and enthusiasts throughout the world.

LYNN SWARD

Tools and Materials

HANDS are the best and favorite tools of any clay artist—but they have their limitations. Before working with clay, wash your hands. You will find that clay easily picks up dust, dirt, and lint from a work surface, your clothing, or your hands.

A ROLLING PIN, BRAYER (a small hand roller with a single handle and available at craft shops), **OR A PASTA MACHINE** can all be used for rolling slabs of clay. Please note: any kitchen tool used for polymer clay should never be used for food preparation.

If you're starting out, buying a pasta machine to use just with clay may be a bigger investment then you're willing to make. You can do everything you need to do with a rolling pin or brayer. As you gain more experience, you may want to buy a pasta machine which will allow you to make uniform-sized slabs quickly and easily.

A SHEET OF GLASS OR PLEXIGLASS makes a perfect, smooth work surface. If you are working on a textured surface, the clay will pick up the imprint—and you may not get the effect you want. Unprotected wood will absorb some of the ingredients of the clay, creating an oily stain. If you must work on unprotected wood, cover your work surface with wax paper. Some clay artists do this no matter what work surface they use since wax paper prevents the clay from sticking and you can easily pick up the sheet of wax paper to move the pieces you make.

A BAKING SHEET AND PARCHMENT PAPER are all you need for baking the clay. Parchment paper prevents the clay from sticking to the baking sheet or from browning on the bottom as it bakes. You can find parchment paper in sheets or in rolls at cooking-supply shops.

CONVENTIONAL OR TOASTER OVENS will bake the clay. Depending on the brand, temperatures for baking range from 215˚ to 275˚F (102˚ to 135˚C). All manufacturers have recommended temperatures for their product. If you bake the clay at higher temperatures than recommended, you will burn the clay and it will emit harmful fumes. If this happens, open the windows and leave the area until the smell is gone.

SHARP SLICING TOOLS such as a craft knife or single-edge razor blade will allow you to make clean, thin slices from the clay. If you are cutting larger slices, a broad-blade scraper with a sharp edge, used for removing wallpaper or paint, will allow you to make thin slices while cutting more area at one time. Experienced clay artists prefer an instrument known as a tissue-slicing tool used in pathology labs. If you can overlook the idea of its intended function, it makes a perfect polymer tool.

CLAY MODELING OR SCULPTING TOOLS will help you when forming the clay. You can find a selection at craft stores or where pottery supplies are sold. One of the tools should be a stylus, either single- or double-edged; this piercing tool will help you make holes for beads as well as give you a sharp point for etching designs. If you are making beads, you may want to bake them on skewers rather than piercing the holes before baking.

A CLAY EXTRUDER allows you to make shapes by pushing the clay through a variety of patterned attachments. When you do this, you will have a long piece of clay that is in the shape of the attachment. You can cut off what you need and save the rest for future projects.

STAMPING DEVICES used for clay work or leather embossing will give texture to the clay if desired. You can also collect objects from around the house as well as from nature that will imprint the clay. Just make sure that whatever you use for imprinting is clean so it will not dirty the clay.

GLUE is necessary for attaching the earring findings. You can use any strong, quick-drying glue. Some manufacturers recommend their own glue brands which are formulated for use with their polymer products. Any cyanoacrylate glue reacts well between metal and polymer. When you glue, make sure you apply the glue to the points of contact. Try to avoid an excess of glue which when dried may come in contact with the earlobe. In some people this may cause an allergic reaction.

MISCELLANEOUS TOOLS AND MATERIALS such as paints, paint brushes, and metallic leaf (see page 000) can help you when you are decorating or embellishing your clay. You can apply leaf directly to clay before baking without using leaf size. For an interesting mottled effect, roll beads in the leaf before baking.

SHEILA SHEPPARD

Getting Started

FIRST, CONDITION YOUR CLAY. Take a small piece of polymer in your hands—it may feel stiff. Some brands have more "body" than others due to advanced formulas for increasing their strength. Knead the clay, pinch it, or roll it. Your body temperature will help soften the clay as you work. You may consider warming the clay slightly before you begin handling it. Some people recommend placing the clay in a plastic bag and putting it in your pocket for a while. Whatever you do to warm it, do not subject the clay to high temperatures or it will begin to harden.

MIXING YOUR OWN COLORS is easy. Just work two or more colors of the conditioned clay until they are blended. If you do not want your colors to mix in a design, start working from the lightest color to the darkest to avoid any color contamination. Experiment making marbled effects with two colors of clay. If you get it just right you'll have swirls of color; if you go too far, the colors will start to blend. Have fun just playing with the clay, since experimentation is your best teacher.

MODELING is one of the easiest ways to work with polymer clay. You can make round or square beads, faces, figures, and objects, using your sculpting tools and hands. If you create a face you like and want to duplicate it, make a press mold. First bake the original face and let it cool. Take a ball of conditioned clay, cut it in half, then press the face into it nose down. Remove the original and bake the impression, allowing it to cool. You now have your mold.

To make your duplicate, brush the inside of the mold lightly with powder, then take a ball of conditioned clay and press it into the mold. Gently remove the impression and bake it.

IRENE DEAN

THIS MODELED PANSY BY LORI BARTHOLOMEW SHOWS THE INDIVIDUAL STEPS THAT GO INTO HER DESIGN.

CANES are logs or loaves of pattern created by bonding shapes and colors of polymer clay together. The idea of caned designs was developed in ancient Egypt for glassmaking. If you've ever seen millefiore glass objects such as beads or paperweights, you've seen examples of the cane technique.

A cane in polymer can be as simple as making a candy cane by rolling two snakes of different colors together, or making a "layer cake" by alternating slabs of two colors (see Figure 1).

More intricate canes, made by combining many different shapes and colors of clay, allow you to create faces, figures, objects, and scenes (see Figure 2).

FIGURE 1. A LAYERED LOAF CAN BE A VERSATILE BASE FOR BUILDING A VARIETY OF CONES.

CONSTRUCT CANES FROM LAYERS
TO CREATE STRIPES AND BLOCKS

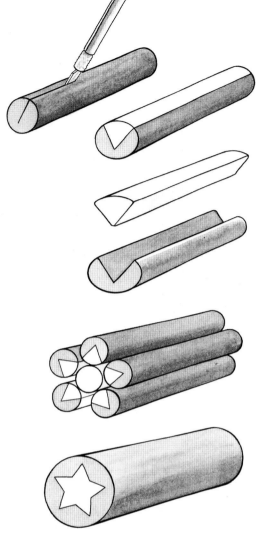

FIGURE 2. A SINGLE-STAR CANE

TO CREATE A CANE, begin by making a colored sketch of your design. Keep it simple. Then divide your conditioned clay as needed, and construct the cane according to the blueprints of your sketch. At this stage, do not be concerned about the size of the cane, work as large as you need while building your design.

Once the design is completed, "reduce" the cane by gently stretching and elongating it until the cane is the size you need. Make sure to work evenly on all sides of the cane as you're reducing. The ends of the cane will get distorted in the process. Don't let this bother you—just keep gently stretching (or rolling evenly if the cane is round). When the cane is the size you want, cut off the ends. You will see a smaller but perfectly proportioned version of your original, larger design.

The magic of canes is that the design is the same no matter where you slice the loaf or roll. You can create one cane and have enough to make many pairs of earrings or other jewelry components. You can reduce a cane to one size, cut off a length, then continue reducing the other piece to get two sizes of the same design. You can cut the cane slices thick or thin. If you have a favorite cane, ration it by cutting it in thin slices, then attach the slices to thicker shapes of solid-color clay. You can also combine different canes for interesting effects.

If you think canes are too complicated and hesitate to attempt them, start simply. The more you work with them, the more confidence you'll develop for trying more complicated designs. If you don't at least experiment with making canes, you're missing one of the greatest features of working with polymer clay.

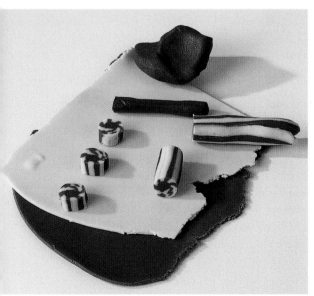

**AN EXAMPLE OF A SIMPLE
JELLY-ROLL CANE**

DESIGNER:
Irene Dean

Playing with Blocks

If you've never worked in polymer clay, start here. It could be your cornerstone to building a whole new addition to your craft knowledge. You won't just gain an introduction to polymer—when you're done, you'll have an attractive pair of earrings to show for it.

MATERIALS

- ¼ block of polymer clay in black
- ¼ block of polymer clay in a color of your choice
- 2 head pins
- Accent beads
- Earring hooks

TOOLS

- Rolling pin or brayer
- Craft knife or single-edge razor blade
- Piercing tool
- Wire cutters
- Round-nose pliers

INSTRUCTIONS

1. Using the rolling pin or brayer, roll two sheets of polymer ¹⁄₁₆ inch (.16 cm) thick, one in black and the other in the color of your choice.

2. Place the black sheet on top of the colored sheet. Use the craft knife or razor blade to cut the sheet into a rectangle measuring at least 2 x 3 inches (5 cm x 7.5 cm).

3. Cut the rectangle into four equal-sized pieces and stack them on top of one another, alternating colors. Press gently to compress the sheets. When you're finished, the block should be about ½ inch (1.5 cm) tall. Let this striped cane rest so slicing does not distort the design.

4. Cut the cane into pieces ¼ inch (.5 cm) square. With the piercing tool, pierce each from top to bottom. Lay on a baking sheet lined with parchment paper and bake according to the manufacturer's instructions.

5. Assemble on a head pin with coordinating beads. Cut the end of the head pin if necessary to ⅛ inch (.3 cm) from the top of the last bead. Using the round-nose pliers, make a loop. Attach the earring finding to this loop.

DESIGNER:
Irene Dean

Seeing Stars

These make a great gift for your favorite "celebrity" or for recognizing a stellar performance or event. You'll learn to make your own hoop for hanging these dazzling easy-to-make stars, a technique you can use for future designs.

MATERIALS

- Polymer clay, small amounts in colors of your choice
- 20-gauge sterling silver wire
- Accent beads for spacers, flat or round

TOOLS

- Rolling pin or brayer
- Pattern cutter with star shape
- Craft knife or single-edge razor blade
- Piercing tool
- Baking sheet
- Parchment paper
- Wire cutters
- ¾-inch (2 cm) dowel
- Round-nose pliers
- Flat-nose pliers
- Emery board or fine file

INSTRUCTIONS

1. Using the rolling pin or brayer, roll polymer clay into sheets about ¹⁄₁₆ inch (.16 cm) thick.

2. With the pattern cutter or working freehand with the craft knife or razor blade, cut star shapes of several sizes.

3. Take the piercing tool and pierce the stars in the center or at the top of one point.

4. Lay the stars on a baking sheet lined with parchment paper and bake according to the manufacturer's instructions. Let cool.

5. Cut a piece of wire about 2¾ inches (7 cm) long. With the round-nose pliers, make an "eye" (loop) on one end. Hold the eye against the dowel and wrap the rest of the wire around the dowel to make a circle. Using a dowel lets you makes a nice round hoop; freehand hoops are never quite as uniform.

6. Assemble the stars on the hoops with spacer beads in between. Put the largest stars on first. For the colored star earrings, use flat silver spacers between the stars and 3mm round beads in the front and back. With the black and white stars, add a silver star charm to the front of the arrangement.

7. When you are satisfied with the arrangement of beads, use flat-nose pliers to turn the last ⅛ inch (.3 cm) of the wire up in a sharp 90° angle so it will fit into the eye on the other end to close the hoop. If the turned-up end of your wire is sharp to the touch, you can smooth it with an emery board or fine file.

DESIGNER:
Susan Kinney

Dancing Man

Use thin slices of a favorite face cane to make bead "heads" for these whimsical dancing figures. Play with different styles of beads for the body, arms, and legs to give your figures their unique character.

MATERIALS

- Polymer clay in colors of your choice
- 2 "head" beads made from face canes
- 2 eye pins
- 8 head pins
- Miscellaneous small beads for neck, hands, feet, and legs
- 2 ear wires
- Quick-drying glue

TOOLS

- Craft knife or single-edge razor blade
- Piercing tool
- Baking sheet
- Parchment paper
- Round-nose pliers
- Wire cutters

INSTRUCTIONS

1. Make your head beads by slicing two thin pieces of the face cane and applying them to two round balls of clay.

2. Using a piercing tool, pierce each head bead, making sure the holes are large enough to accommodate the eye pins. Place the beads on a baking sheet lined with parchment paper and bake according to the manufacturer's instructions. Let cool.

3. Insert an eye pin into the top of each head bead (with the eye of the eye pin at the top of the head), and string on a small bead for the neck.

4. Make two "arms" by stringing two head pins with star beads for the hands and long bugle or tube beads for the arms. Clip the ends of the head pins if necessary and make loops. Try to make all your hand-formed loops as small as possible. String the arms onto the eye pin.

5. String the larger round "body" beads onto the eye pin. Clip the ends of the eye pin if necessary and make a neat loop at the base of each body bead.

6. Make the "legs" by stringing two head pins with small round beads for the feet and bugle or tube beads for the legs. Make loops at the end of the head pins.

7. Attach the legs to the loop you made at the base of the body bead.

8. Attach the ear wires to the loop at the top of the head bead.

9. If desired, add a drop of glue to the arm joints to keep the arms extended.

after a fashion

Earrings have always been subject to the whims of changing hairstyles and headwear. Roman matrons for instance could continue to exhibit their large earrings because their upswept hair did not encumber them. In the Middle Ages and into the early and mid-Renaissance elaborate headdresses either prevented women from wearing any earrings or allowed them to wear only the smallest, simplest hoops.

Toward the end of the Renaissance hair was parted in the middle and worn either loose or fixed in simple braids and knots that exposed the ears. Large earrings became popular and served to balance the look of tightly corseted gowns made of heavily embroidered brocade.

The girandole evolved as an earring style that could accommodated the elaborate hairdos and plunging necklines popular in the eighteenth century. Girandoles were a variation on a design that consisted of a bow or bow-inspired motif made of gold or silver set with precious stones to which three large stones or pearls were suspended.

This style could be very heavy and often had to be made with a fitting that enabled women to distribute the weight of the earring by means of a ribbon that they could thread over the ear and into the hair. The girandole was so popular that many women who could not afford expensive jewelry copied the style by simply tying a bow from ribbons they had threaded through their pierced lobes.

As hair styles and wigs escalated to giddy extremes in the eighteenth century, the girandole evolved into the pendeloque. This design had a much longer vertical drop that complemented fashion's elongated lines. Perhaps one of the last big influences of hat and hair on earrings was in the mid-nineteenth century when hair was worn low over the ears and bonnets were an integral part of fashionable dress.

In this century the bobbed hair of the 20s gave way to the pixie cuts of the 50s with many of today's women opting for the time-saving convenience of shorter hair. Now it's much more common to see a woman wearing a hat out of necessity to protect her from the sun or keep her head warm then it is to see a hat as part of a matched ensemble.

While earring design will always be linked to the styles of the day, earrings have emerged as accessories that can stand on their own. Since modern women no longer slavishly follow fashion dictates, they have developed a relaxed style with an emphasis on individual expression. By selecting an outfit to show off a unique pair of treasured earrings women continue to assert their rights to make their own fashion statement.

DESIGNER:
Irene Dean

Cunning Cane Tubes

You can't disguise the fact that canes are versatile polymer clay creations. Because the design of a cane runs its length, you can use as much or as little as you want simply by cutting it thick or thin. This design shows you how to make tube beads from a favorite cane, giving you a variety of earring options.

MATERIALS

- ⅛ block of polymer clay
- One or more prepared canes
- Accent beads
- Head pins
- Ear wires or finding of your choice

TOOLS

- Long needle or skewer
- Cutting blade—wallpaper scrapers with their broad, flat, sharp blades make good cutting tools for polymer clay
- Baking sheet
- Parchment paper
- Round-nose pliers

INSTRUCTIONS

1. Using your hands, roll a piece of polymer clay into a ball about ½ inch (1.5 cm) in diameter. Use scrap clay if you plan to cover it entirely with cane slices; use a solid color if you want it to show in between the cane.

2. Pierce the ball of clay with the long needle or skewer, moving the ball to the approximate center of the skewer. Keeping the ball on the skewer, make a snake by carefully rolling the ball between your work surface and your hand. If the polymer becomes too loose on the skewer, gently twist and squeeze the clay until it tightens on the skewer again. Then roll it on your work surface to smooth it. Try to make the tube of clay a consistent diameter about ¼ inch (.5 cm) thick. Cut off the distorted ends.

3. Using a sharp cutting blade, cut thin slices from one or more prepared canes. Keep in mind the finished length you want for your beads as you arrange the slices onto the polymer snake. Leave space between each slice or butt the edges together.

4. Gently roll the snake of polymer, with the skewer still inside, back and forth on your work surface. Apply enough pressure with your hands to smooth the cane designs into the background but not so much as to distort the images.

5. Make individual beads by cutting them from the length of the snake. Begin by pressing your blade into the polymer snake and pushing it forward on your work surface so the clay and skewer roll under the blade. Proceed around the snake carefully so the blade finds the beginning of the cut you've made. Repeat cutting the size beads you want on the length of the snake until you've cut all the beads you need. Do not remove the beads from the skewer.

6. Place the cut beads that are still on the skewer on a baking sheet lined with parchment paper. Bake according to manufacturer's instructions. Allow to cool, then remove the beads from the skewer.

7. The skewer method results in more uniform beads without the distortion caused by piercing each bead individually. However, you could also make tube-shaped beads without using the skewer inside. Follow the above steps, disregarding the skewer instructions. After cutting the cane-covered snake into individual beads, pierce each with a straight pin or awl to make a hole.

8. Assemble the earrings by placing the polymer beads onto the head pins with accent beads. Cut the end of the head pin so there is a ⅛-inch (.3 cm) end coming from the top of the last bead. Use the round-nose pliers to make a loop, then attach the ear wires to this loop.

DESIGNER:
Lynn Sward

Shimmering Shapes

A dusting of colored metallic powders lends a glittering surface to these embossed shapes. They look terrific and are easy to make.

MATERIALS

- Paper or thin cardboard
- Pro-Mat or other strong polymer clay in colors of your choice
- Metallic powders
- Matte varnish in a can or spray
- Strong, quick-drying glue—cyanoacrylate glues react best between metal and polymer
- Ear findings

TOOLS

- Pencil
- Rolling pin, brayer, or pasta machine
- Craft knife or single-edge razor blade
- Artist's brushes
- Protective mask
- Commercial embossing or stamping tools—or make your own using any raised designs you like that will imprint the clay
- Baking sheet
- Parchment paper

INSTRUCTIONS

1. Design the shapes for your earrings and make a pattern using paper or cardboard.

2. Roll your clay until you have a slab that is approximately ⅛ inch (.3 cm) thick.

3. Lay your pattern on the clay and cut out the shapes of your earrings.

4. Apply the metallic powders, using a brush or your fingers. Experiment. You may want your clay color to show through, or you may want to cover the entire surface with the powders. *Note:* Follow the manufacturer's safety precautions for using metallic powders. It is advisable to to wear a disposable painter's protective mask (an allergy mask) when working.

5. Stamp your design. You may also try stamping your design first, then applying the metallic powders for a different effect.

6. Lay the earrings on a baking sheet lined with parchment paper. Place the baking sheet in a cold oven. Set the oven at 265°F (130°C) and bake for 25 minutes. Allow to cool.

7. Apply a fine matte varnish to the earrings.

8. Attach your findings using a quick-drying strong glue. Cyanoacrylate glues react best with metal and polymer

Variations

Incorporate metallic powders and embossing into projects using the techniques for the project found on page 54.

DESIGNER:
Irene Dean

Swirls and Twirls

Here is a way to conserve a special cane or to combine cane slices. You may get better results if you use one of the stronger polymer clays, such as Fimo, Cernit, or Pro-Mat. This project is best worked on a sheet of waxed paper. Instead of having to scrape the polymer from your work surface, you can simply peel the waxed paper off the back.

MATERIALS

- ¼ block polymer clay
- One or two canes
- 2 eye pins
- 2 earring hooks

TOOLS

- Flat-nose pliers
- Waxed paper
- Rolling pin or brayer
- Craft knife or single-edge razor blade

INSTRUCTIONS

1. Use the flat-nose pliers to bend two eye pins into curvy zigzags about ½ inch (1.5 cm) long. Flatten them by placing the zigzags in the jaws of the pliers and squeezing. The curves will prevent the eye pin from being pulled out of the clay.

2. On the wax paper, flatten approximately ¼ block of polymer clay into a sheet approximately ⅛ inch (.3 cm) thick. Cut into two pieces.

3. Place each eye pin on one of the sheets of polymer so the eye hangs over the edge. Use a brayer or rolling pin and roll over the eye pins until they are embedded in the polymer clay and even with the surface.

4. Take the canes you will use and, with a very sharp blade, cut thin slices. You may use one special cane, such as a face or very complex image, or you may want to combine canes, such as a few leaves and a flower, or several jelly rolls or other simple designs.

5. Arrange the slices on the sheets of polymer over the eye pins. Be sure to cover the eye pins completely with your cane slices. Make sure the eye of each eye pin is at the center of the top of your arrangement.

6. Roll over the design with your brayer or rolling pin so the cane slices are rolled into the sheet of polymer that is underneath them. You may want to put a piece of waxed paper over the design to keep it from picking up any stray polymer pieces that may stick to your brayer.

7. If you've used the wax paper for a top sheet, remove it. Then use the craft knife or single-edge razor blade to cut around the perimeter of the cane designs. Remove the excess clay.

8. Carefully peel the waxed paper backing from the polymer, using your fingers to smooth the edges of the earring designs. You may need to use an awl or needle tool to clear away any clay that was pushed into the eyes of the eye pins.

9. Place the earrings on a baking sheet lined with parchment paper. Bake according to manufacturer's instructions. Allow to cool.

10. Attach ear wires or findings of your choice to the eye of the eye pin. To prevent putting stress on the earring designs, open the loops on the ear wires or findings instead of opening the loops on the eye pins.

DESIGNER:
Lynn Sward

Picture This

If there's a special fabric or graphic that's caught your eye, you can turn it into an earring. Translucent polymer seals the print of your choice to give you a colorful, almost instant, conversation piece.

MATERIALS

- Pro-Mat or other strong polymer clay—this is a strong formula, preferred for its extra body
- Fabric or graphic of choice
- Cardboard
- White craft glue
- Metallic leaf
- Translucent (clear) polymer clay
- Extra fine sandpaper, 000 grit
- Coarse sandpaper, 60 grit
- Ear posts
- Strong, quick-drying glue— look for cyanoacrylate glue since it reacts best when gluing metal to polymer

TOOLS

- Scissors
- Copy machine
- Rolling pin, brayer, or pasta machine
- Craft knife, or single-edge razor blade
- Tissue blade—a surgical instrument with a very thin blade (you can also use a craft knife with fine blade)
- Baking sheet
- Parchment paper
- Oven
- Motorized craft tool with buffer wheel attachment

INSTRUCTIONS

1. Choose a colorful fabric or graphic. Do not be concerned about the scale of the design.

2. Take the fabric or graphic to a copy shop. Reducing the size of the original, make a color copy of the fabric or graphic. You may need to make several copies until you get the print to the size you want.

3. Take a small square of cardboard approximately 4 x 4 inches (10 x 10 cm). Cut out a square "window" approximately 2 x 2 inches (5 cm x 5 cm) from the center of the larger cardboard square.

4. Move the window over the color copy until you find an area of the design you like the best. This will be the part of the design you will use for your earring. Cut out two of these areas.

5. With cardboard, make a pattern for the earring. This should be the exact size and shape you want for the design. Keep in mind that the finished earring will be $1/8$ inch (.3 cm) larger around the edges. Using the pattern, cut out your copied color design.

7. Using a rolling pin, brayer, or pasta machine, roll a slab of clay until it is approximately $1/8$ inch (.3 cm) thick. If you're using a pasta machine, roll the clay first on the number one setting, then roll it twice on the number three setting. Make the slab large enough to cut two earrings.

8. Lay the cutout designs on the clay slab. Using a craft knife, cut the clay approximately $1/8$ inch (.3 cm) from the edge of the paper.

9. Glue the paper to the clay using a few drops of white glue, maintaining the $1/8$-inch (.3 cm) edge.

10. Using the tissue blade, or craft knife with a very fine blade, cut a paper-thin slice from a piece of clay. *Be extra cautious when using any sharp instruments!* Apply metallic leaf to the surface of the thin clay slab and fix it to the surface by pressing gently with your fingers or rolling lightly with the rolling pin or brayer.

11. With a craft knife, cut out small pieces of the metallic slab and apply to the earrings to highlight the design. You want these to be paper-thin because you do not want any raised areas on your design.

12. Using the rolling pin, brayer, or pasta machine, roll a slab of translucent clay approximately $1/16$ inch (.16 cm) thick. If you are using the pasta machine, first roll it on the number one setting, then on number six, and finally on number seven.

13. Lay the translucent slab on top of the earring. Using a craft knife, cut around the edges.

14. Lay the earrings on a baking sheet lined with parchment paper.

15. Place the baking sheet in a cold oven. Set the oven at 265°F (130°C). *Note:* Through trial and error, this temperature seems to be the best for baking translucent clay and will prevent it from turning dark. Take the earrings out of the oven after 25 minutes and let cool. If you see the ends curling up once the earrings have been cooling for a time, take heavy books and place them on the earrings. Make sure that the cover of the book that comes in contact with the earring is smooth so no texture imprints the clay.

16. When the earrings are completely dry, sand the surface lightly with the fine 000 sandpaper.

17. Using the motorized craft tool with the buffer wheel attachment, buff the surface to a nice gloss. You can buff by hand but will not get as high a gloss.

18. Glue the posts to the backs of the earrings. If you sand the finding before gluing, you will get a better bond. Let the glue set at least two hours before wearing.

DESIGNER:
Susan Kinney

African Swirls

You can get an almost infinite variety of effects in polymer by experimenting with canes made of "cakes" and "snakes." With different colors of clay and other styles of purchased beads, you can create a multitude of earrings following the same basic instructions. For extra drama, try using three dangles.

MATERIALS

- Polymer clay in brown, ivory, and black
- 2 head pins
- Small glass and matte beads
- 2, 12-14mm brass African beads
- 2 post backs or clips with loops for attaching a dangle—both available where earring findings are sold
- Quick-drying glue

TOOLS

- Rolling pin, brayer, or pasta machine
- Piercing tool
- Baking sheet
- Parchment paper
- Round-nose pliers
- Wire cutters

INSTRUCTIONS

See pages 44–45 for how-tos on making simple canes.

1. Roll each color of clay into slabs approximately 1/16 inch (.16 cm) thick.

2. Construct two "cake" canes by layering alternating colors into a block.

3. Roll one cane (make a "snake") into a swirl pattern—making a "jelly roll" cane. Cut this rolled cane in half and set aside.

4. Slice the other cane into stacked slices (see Figure 1 on page 44). Gently roll the stacked slices until they make a slab that is large enough to wrap around the circumference of one of the jelly rolls. Don't roll the slab too thin.

5. Wrap the layered cane around one half of the jelly roll cane. Reduce this cane until it is approximately ¾ inch (2 cm) in diameter. Slice two pieces for the earring tops.

6. Reduce the other half of the jelly roll cane from Step 2 to approximately ½ inch (1.5 cm) in diameter. Slice this reduced cane into pieces that are ¼ inch (.5 cm) thick.

7. Using a piercing tool, make a hole in the ¼-inch (.5 cm) slices running from top to bottom. Make the holes large enough to accommodate the head pins.

8. Place the pieces on a baking sheet that has been lined with parchment paper, and bake according to the manufacture's instructions.

9. String a combination of the small glass and matte beads with your handmade "swirl" beads in a pleasing arrangement on the head pins. For an interesting look, make an asymmetrical pair.

10. Clip the head pins, leaving enough for the loops. Using the round-nose pliers, make the loops.

11. Glue the earring backs or clips with loops for attaching dangles onto a large flat polymer swirl bead.

12. Attach the head pin dangle to the loop on the earring back.

Variations

- Play with the "cakes" and "snakes" to make more intricate designs.

- Reduce pieces of the canes into even smaller sizes for accent beads.

- Take a slice of a large cane and cut a hole from the middle to make a Pi ring for hanging.

- Use waxed linen cord for stringing the dangles instead of a head pin.

be bold

Men are reclaiming their earring heritage. You are almost as likely to see a small gold hoop or solitaire on a young businessman as on a retired grandfather. This is not a new phenomenon.

Statues from antiquity show gods and kings with pierced, adorned lobes. A fad of the Renaissance led men to wear the shoelaces of their ladyloves in their pierced ears. It is thought that a lady placed the shoelaces in her lover's earlobes to announce a betrothal.

Noblemen of the sixteenth and seventeenth century wore a fraction of their wealth on their ears as they preened and fawned through the courts of Europe. French military officers of the eighteenth century sported earrings along with their medals, sabers, and boots.

Sailors, in homage to Poseidon who was often depicted in paintings and statues as wearing earrings, traditionally pierced one earlobe to mark their first crossing of the equator, rounding of the horn of Africa, or to generally keep them safe from drowning.

Gardener's Delight

Flowerpots and ladybugs bring to mind quiet times in the potting shed. If you like to garden, show the world with these charming miniatures.

Flowerpots

MATERIALS

- Polymer clay in these colors:
  - Red
  - Orange
  - Yellow
  - Blue pearlized
  - Yellow pearlized
- 2 ear posts or clip backs
- Adhesive or glue (E-6000 works well with polymer)

TOOLS

- Small kitchen knife
- Parchment paper
- Baking sheet
- Rolling pin
- Double-sided stylus
- Regular or toaster oven

INSTRUCTIONS

1. Knead small amounts of red, orange, and yellow polymer until you get a terra-cotta color.

2. Using this terra-cotta clay, roll a ball the size of a marble. With the kitchen knife, cut the ball in half and shape each half into the pot shape (wider at the top, tapered toward the bottom). Lay the flowerpots on a baking sheet lined with parchment paper.

3. Using a rolling pin, flatten a marble-sized, terra-cotta colored ball of clay. From it, cut four strips 1½ inches (4 cm) long by ¼ inch (.5 cm) wide.

4. Lay one strip of clay against the top edge of each of the flowerpots. Trim the excess strip of clay evenly with the back of each pot.

5. Lay one strip of clay against the bottom edge of each pot. Trim the excess strip evenly with the back of each pot.

6. To make the blue flowers, use the blue pearlized clay and roll 20 small balls the size of mustard seeds (tiny). Arrange the balls in circles of five to resemble four five-petaled flowers.

7. Position the flowers on the flowerpots as shown. When the flowers are in place, use the large end of a double-ended stylus to make indentations in each petal.

8. To make the flower centers, use yellow pearlized clay to form 10 balls the size of mustard seeds. Attach these centers to each flower using light finger pressure.

9. Bake the earrings at 275°F (135°C) for 15 minutes. When they have cooled completely, remove them from the baking sheet.

10. Apply the adhesive to the ear post or clip backs, then attach to the earrings by positioning them to the center backs.

Ladybugs

MATERIALS

- Red and black polymer clay
- Metallic silver acrylic paint
- Clear gloss acrylic spray
- Adhesive (E-6000 works well with polymer)
- Ear posts or clip backs

TOOLS

- Parchment paper
- Baking sheet
- Ruler
- Crochet hook, #9 (US)
- Double-ended stylus
- Regular or toaster oven

INSTRUCTIONS

1. Take the black clay and roll two balls the size of small marbles. Flatten each ball between your thumb and index finger, creating two ½-inch x ½-inch x ¼-inch (1.5 x 1.5 x .5 cm) oval-shaped "bodies." Lay them on a baking sheet lined with parchment paper.

2. Using the black clay, roll two balls the size of small peas. Gently press one of the small balls onto the top of each oval, creating the heads.

3. Using the red clay, make two pairs of wings following the pattern. Lay the wings on top of the body as shown, pressing down gently to adhere.

4. Using the hook end of a #9 (US) crochet hook, begin at the head-end of the ladybugs and lightly score the red clay wings using downward strokes.

5. With the black clay, roll 14 balls the size of mustard seeds. Position seven of them on each of the ladybug's wings as shown, pressing gently to adhere.

6. Using the large end of the double-ended stylus, make two impressions in each ladybug's head to resemble eyes.

7. Bake earrings at 275°F (135°C) for 15 minutes. When the earrings have cooled completely, remove from the baking sheet.

8. Using the large end of the double-ended stylus, dip the stylus into the metallic silver paint. Fill the impressions on each head (the "eyes") with the paint. Allow the paint to dry thoroughly.

9. Seal the ladybugs using clear gloss acrylic spray, first spraying the tops, letting them dry, then spraying the backs.

10. Apply the adhesive to the ear posts or clip backs, then attach them by positioning them to the center backs of the earrings.

DESIGNER:
Sheila Sheppard

New Age Stone Age

Possibly the perfect earrings for any armchair archeologist. Create an ancient look with one of the newest and easiest-to-use craft materials. The polymer clay "stone" earrings have the look of old, hand-carved, rock beads. The black pair feature "etching" that is really a thin layer of a simple cane. Be adventurous, experiment until you get the look you want.

Stone Earrings

MATERIALS

- Polymer clay in these colors:
  - Translucent
  - Mint
  - Aqua
  - Copper
  - Ivory
  - Brown
  - Purple
  - Yellow
- 2, 3-inch (7.5 cm) silver head pins
- Assorted small glass beads
- Disk beads
- Silver jewelry wire
- Silver ear wires or clip backs

TOOLS

- Craft knife or single-edge razor
- Assorted sculpting or modeling tools
- Materials for texturing, such as fabric, wire mesh, and stamps
- Piercing tool—metal stylus with sharp end
- Baking sheet
- Parchment paper
- Round-nose pliers
- Needle-nose pliers

INSTRUCTIONS

1. Begin by mixing small bits of colored clay into proportionately greater amounts of translucent clay. Do not blend the colors completely. Tear, pinch, or cut these batches apart. Press them together enough to bond, but do not press them too tightly. Create several rectangular and square bead shapes. Don't try to make duplicate pieces; this will give them a more natural look.

2. Using modeling tools or textured materials such as stamps, fabric, or wire mesh, create textured surfaces on the stones.

3. Pierce the shapes to make holes for stringing. You can also leave an oven-proof skewer in the pieces while they bake.

4. Place the shapes on a baking sheet that you've lined with parchment paper.

5. Bake at 275°F (135°C) for 15 minutes (or follow the manufacturer's instructions). Allow to cool.

6. Take two head pins, string on a small glass bead. Assemble your stones according to your design. You may want to use small disks in between the stones or make your own coordinating disk beads out of the clay. Leave enough room, approximately ¾ inch (2 cm), at the end of the head pin for making a loop.

7. Using the round-nose pliers, make a loop from the end of the head pin. For a more finished look, use the needle-nose pliers to wrap jewelry wire around the base of the loop you just made.

8. Insert an ear wire or attach a clip back.

Etched Earrings

MATERIALS

- Polymer clay in these colors:
  - Black
  - Ivory
  - Turquoise
- 2, 3-inch (7.5 cm) silver head pins
- 2 thin twigs, 1¼ inch (3 cm) long
- 2 flat silver disk beads
- Assorted small beads
- Silver ear wires

TOOLS

- Rolling pin or brayer
- Craft knife or single-edge razor
- Assorted sculpting or modeling tools
- Baking sheet
- Parchment paper
- Round-nose pliers

INSTRUCTIONS

1. With the rolling pin or brayer, make several sheets each of black and ivory colored clay. Alternate sheets to make a striped rectangular cane. You will use this for the etching. Again using the black and ivory in alternating layers, make a small jelly roll cane. This is for the decorative circle at the top of the bead.

2. With the black polymer, roll two 2-inch (5 cm) long pencil-thick beads.

3. Insert a 3-inch (7.5 cm) head pin in each bead, with the flat end of the head pin at the bottom of the bead. This will imbed the head pin in the bead since you will bake the bead with the head pin in it.

4. Take small bits of turquoise clay and place them according to your design. Use the modeling tool to pack a small amount of black clay around the head of the pin at the bottom to hide the head.

5. With a razor blade or craft knife, make two paper-thin slices of the striped cane. Lay one slice over each bead and gently roll the cane onto the surface of the beads.

6. Determine which side of the beads will be the front and back. Gently flatten the side that will be the back.

7. Take two small twigs, approximately 1¼ inches (3 cm) long. Make two thin snakes of translucent clay, then wrap the snakes around the twigs.

8. On the front of each bead, use a modeling tool to make small depressions the length of the twigs. Lay the twigs with the snakes into each depression. Press the twig gently at each end to secure.

9. Make two thin slices of the jelly roll cane. Using a sculpting tool, press one on each bead above the twigs. If necessary, wrap a small piece of black clay around the top of the head pin, leaving approximately a ¾-inch (2 cm) end on the head pin for making the loop.

10. Lay the beads on a baking sheet lined with parchment paper and bake at 275°F (135°C) for 15 minutes (or follow the manufacturer's instructions). Allow to cool.

11. String the disk beads on the head pins, adding additional beads if desired.

12. Using the round-nose pliers, make a loop on the end of the head pin. Insert the ear wires into the loop.

DESIGNER:
Lori Bartholomew

Rose Trellis

You can almost smell the roses. A touch of metallic paint highlights this delicate trellis and rose design, recalling the soft light of an early summer morning.

MATERIALS

- Polymer clay in these colors:
  - White pearlized *(pearlized clay contains an additive which gives it a shimmering appearance)*
  - Blue pearlized
  - Pink pearlized
  - Yellow pearlized
  - Leaf green
- Metallic copper acrylic paint
- Adhesive or glue (E-6000 works well with polymer)
- Ear posts or clip backs

TOOLS

- Rolling pin
- Small kitchen knife
- Baking sheet
- Parchment paper
- Ruler
- Double-edged stylus or toothpicks
- Regular or toaster oven
- Small artist's paintbrush
- Paper towel

INSTRUCTIONS

1. Using the white clay, form two balls the size of large marbles. Roll the clay with the rolling pin to a thickness of ⅛ inch (.3 cm). Using the kitchen knife, cut 12 strips, each 1¼ inch (3 cm) long by ⅛ inch (.3 cm) wide.

2. Lay three strips diagonally on a baking sheet lined with parchment paper, leaving a ⅛-inch (.3 cm) space between each strip. Weave the remaining strips in an over-under fashion, leaving ⅛ inch (.3 cm) between each strip.

3. Trim the sides of the trellis until it measures 1 inch (2.5 cm) square. Repeat this procedure for the second trellis:

4. Using the leaf green clay, cut six strips in the shape of narrow leaves. Make two leaves ½ inch (1.5 cm) long and four leaves ¼ inch (.5 cm) long. Apply the leaves to the lattice, positioning the longest leaf in the center and the two shorter leaves on either side.

5. To make the small blue flowers, take the blue clay and form 50 balls the size of mustard seeds. Arrange five balls in a cluster resembling a five-petal flower. Position the clusters on the trellis over the leaves. When the flowers are in place, use the large end of a double-ended stylus and make indentations in each petal. Using the yellow clay, form ten balls the size of mustard seeds. Apply the centers to each flower by using light finger pressure.

6. To make the rose, begin by taking the pink clay and rolling two balls the size of small peas. Press one of the balls between your index finger and thumb to form a thin, flat rectangle. Beginning at the right end of the rectangle, roll the clay gently toward the left edge to form a center for the rose. Do the same with the other ball.

7. Roll six smaller balls and flatten each one between your thumb and index finger to form the rose petals. Apply each of the three petals to the bud. Gently curl the edges of each petal between the thumb and index finger to create a natural-looking rose. Cut away the excess clay from behind the completed rose. Using the smaller end of a double-ended stylus, or a toothpick, gently press the rose into place on the bottom of the trellis.

8. Roll four small balls, then follow the directions for making the rose center in Step 6 to create four small rosebuds. Position the rosebuds with a stylus or toothpick at right angles behind the roses.

9. Bake the earrings at 275°F (135°C) for 15 minutes. When the earrings have cooled completely, remove them from the baking sheet.

10. You want only a hint of paint on the finished piece to give it an antiqued look. You can accomplish this by working with a "dry brush" technique. To do this, first dip your paint brush in the metallic copper paint, then brush it on a dry paper towel several times to remove most of the paint. Brush the remaining paint lightly over the surface of the earrings. Paint each flower center with the metallic copper paint.

11. Apply an adhesive or glue to the ear posts or clip backs and position them at the top and center of each trellis.

DESIGNER:
Susan Kinney

Face It!

Immortalize a fascinating face from old jewelry, small statues, or dolls by turning them into a pair of earrings. You can also use your own sculpted creations. By using a press mold you can make multiple earrings to give as gifts.

MATERIALS

- Small faces for casting— or sculpt your own
- Polymer clay in pale green turquoise
- Polymer clay in colors of your choice
- White and brown acrylic paint
- Cyanoacrylate glue, or strong, quick-drying glue
- Earring backs or clips

TOOLS

- Baking sheet
- Parchment paper
- Artist's brush
- Cotton swabs
- Lint-free rags

INSTRUCTIONS

1. Follow the directions on page 42 for making and using a press mold. Mold the face of your choice and "cast" two of these, using a pleasing color mixture of polymer clay.

2. Place the faces on a baking sheet that has been lined with parchment paper. Bake the clay according to the manufacturer's instructions. Allow to cool.

3. With your fingertip, brush, or cotton swab, apply brown paint to the faces. Immediately wipe off the surface, leaving "shadows" in the face hollows. Let dry.

4. To create a slightly antiqued face, apply white paint over the faces and wipe off the excess. Let dry.

5. Using the glue, apply the earring backs or clips.

Variations

Experiment with different faces, colors of clay, and paint colors. A small version of these faces could be used as a head for a "dancing man pin" or earrings (see page 48).

F A B R I C
P A P E R and
M I X E D
M E D I A

In exploring potential for new designs, look to materials not traditionally associated with the object you're creating. While it's logical to consider polymer clay, beads, and metal when thinking about earrings, what about fabric, paper, metallic leaf, old photos, or cardboard? By expanding your outlook, you'll enlarge your possibilities. For all you know, you can have the makings of a great pair of earrings hanging in your closet or sitting in your desk drawer.

PEI-LING BECKER

LEIGH McADAMS

Tools and Materials

A PAIR OF SCISSORS, A CRAFT KNIFE, A UTILITY KNIFE, SINGLE-EDGE RAZOR BLADES, or a rotary cutter used for cutting fabric are all basic tools to consider when working with fabric and paper. You'll also want to keep your basic pliers handy (see page 9) to help you attach the findings or for looping a head pin.

ARTIST'S BRUSHES and disposable foam brushes are necessary for painting. To help eliminate mess, use disposable paper plates as palettes for mixing paint. Lint-free rags are always useful. Save your screw-top jars for mixing dyes or storing lacquers.

MAT BOARD, used for framing and mounting pictures and prints, is an ideal weight for making earrings. It is thicker and more dense than other cardboards and usually has a slightly textured surface. Handmade decorative papers are also a beautiful addition to your earrings. The variety of color and textures will inspire you.

ACRYLIC PAINTS are suitable for paper and fabric. They are water soluble, providing a quick cleanup. To add raised details to the surface of your earrings, use dimensional "puffy" paints. They are easy to apply from their own disposable bottles and can be found in a range of colors including metallics. You may want to have some permanent markers with fine points on hand for highlighting. Markers with metallic inks are great for adding a touch of sparkle with a gilded look.

LACQUER, VARNISH, OR GLOSS MEDIUM are used to seal paper and fabric once you've made your earrings; this will protect them and give them a gloss or matte finish. Gloss medium, for use with acrylic paints, is water soluble and needs to be applied with a brush. Lacquer and varnish come in cans for applying with a brush or as spray preparations. There are other spray formulas available at art-supply and craft shops that will also work to seal your earrings. When using a spray it's better to apply several light coats, allowing each coat to dry thoroughly. This will prevent drips that can ruin your work.

GLUE for making fabric and paper earrings can be as simple as white craft glue or white glue suitable for fabric. Some designers prefer the quick-dry glue for fixing buttons, beads, and other decorative additions to their earrings.

FUSIBLE WEB, an iron-on facing material for sewing, is another way to fix fabric to other earring materials. You'll be most successful if you iron the fabric and web on a flat surface, then cut out your shapes.

METALLIC LEAF can be an attractive addition to your earring design. It's thin sheets of metal used for covering surfaces or embellishing designs. You can find metallic leaf in gold, silver, copper, and variegated colors at art- or craft- supply shops.

You buy leaf in "books" containing 25 sheets of leaf that are separated by tissue paper. Because leaf is so thin, keep the leaf between two pieces of tissue paper when you cut or tear it. When you lay the leaf, it's much easier to pick up the pieces of leaf with the tissue paper rather than handling it directly with you fingers.

To fix the leaf to the surface, you need to apply "leaf size" (available where you buy leaf) to the area of the design you want "gilded." Allow the size to dry until it is tacky (slightly sticky) to the touch. Pick up the leaf with the tissue paper, and lay the leaf on the sized area. Let the leaf "rest" (dry) for several hours, then use a stiff artist's brush to gently brush away any excess leaf.

MISCELLANEOUS TREASURES can be fixed to your earrings to enhance your design. Buttons, charms, and meaningful mementos are easily applied with glue and can add a sentimental touch to your earrings.

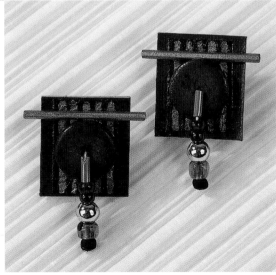

PEI-LING BECKER

DESIGNER:
Mary Scott Hoyt

Quilts

Colorful quilt patterns are the source of inspiration for these designs. By using a special plastic that reduces in size when heated in an oven, you can create captivating miniatures without straining your eyes.

MATERIALS

- Book with quilt patterns for ideas
- PolyShrink sheet
- Very fine wet/dry sandpaper
- Acrylic paint or high-quality colored pencils
- Large permanent marker
- Extra fine point permanent marker in black
- Jump rings
- Beads
- Eye pins
- Earring findings

TOOLS

- Sharp scissors
- Artist's brushes
- Hole punch
- Nonstick cookie sheet
- Conventional oven
- Round-nose pliers
- Needle-nose pliers

INSTRUCTIONS

1. For inspiration, spend time with a good quilt book. Decide on a quilt pattern for your design.

2. Using the very fine wet/dry sandpaper, sand the plastic sheet crisscross (diagonally in one direction, then diagonally in the other direction). Sand thoroughly.

3. Trace or draw the quilt pattern on the plastic. Since the plastic will shrink 50%, you may want to experiment with baking a variety of designs until you feel comfortable with the finished proportions.

4. Cut out two "quilts." If you are making a square quilt, you may want to cut off the tips of the four corners before baking to prevent them from being too sharp.

5. Paint the back of the cutout quilts. You may use black or a color of your choice. A large permanent marker works well for this step.

6. Paint your design with acrylic paint that you have slightly thinned with water, or use colored pencils.

7. When the paint is completely dry, add details with a brush or extra fine point magic marker.

8. With the hole punch, make a hole at the top of each earring.

9. Lay the pieces on a nonstick baking sheet. Bake in a conventional oven at 275°F (135°C) for two to five minutes. Allow to cool completely.

10. You can finish your earring in several ways. You can simply insert a jump ring into the hole, then attach your earring finding. Or, you can thread an eye pin with beads. Then insert a jump ring into the hole of the earring and attach the eye of the eye pin to the jump ring. Using the round-nose pliers, make a loop on the end of the eye pin for attaching your finding.

Another method is to thread a length of jewelry wire into the hole in the earring. Then using the needle-nose pliers, decoratively twist or wrap the wire. Thread on beads and make a loop at the end of the wire for attaching your finding using the round-nose pliers.

THINK BIG
using PolyShrink

If you like the look of miniatures but have trouble working in such small scale, you may want to investigate PolyShrink. You can work big to produce smaller, lightweight pieces—perfect for earrings!

Available in sheets, this flexible plastic reduces 50% in size when baked in a conventional oven (not microwave). Plan ahead to make any holes you need for inserting jump rings and findings. Before baking, you can use scissors to cut PolyShrink or use a paper punch to make holes. Afterwards, since baking makes it rigid, you will need to use a small saw or file to cut and shape your pieces. Once baked, the pieces will be approximately $1/16$ inch (.16 cm) thick.

Because it has a smooth surface, you must sand the plastic before applying any medium. To create your designs you can use markers, inks, colored pencils, or paint directly on the sanded plastic sheet. Always let paint dry thoroughly before baking. Since PolyShrink is baked at 275˚F (135˚C), make sure that whatever medium you use can tolerate that temperature.

DESIGNER:
Peggy DeBell

Photo Earrings

Lockets were once a favorite way to keep a portrait of a loved one close to your heart. With these photo earrings, you have a new way to show the world exactly who (or what!) you hold most dear.

MATERIALS

- Black-and-white photos developed on a contact sheet
- Cotton fabric
- Fabric paint in black and white
- Iron-on fusible web (used for fusing (bonding) fabric)
- Watercolor board, medium weight
- Clear acrylic spray
- Fabric glue
- Dimensional "puffy" fabric paint in silver
- French ear wires

TOOLS

- Scissors
- Artist's paintbrush
- Iron
- Small hand drill or small craft drill
- Rotary fabric cutter

INSTRUCTIONS

1. Take black-and-white photos of your favorite subjects. When you take the film to the photo shop, ask that they be developed on a contact sheet. When you get them back, all the photos from that roll of film will be on one sheet of paper. You can cut up the contact sheet, choosing the exposures you want for the earrings.

2. Paint a small piece of cotton fabric with black and white fabric paint. Let it dry thoroughly, then iron it flat.

3. Using the iron and the fusible web, fuse the fabric to the watercolor board by following the manufacturer's instructions.

4. Paint the back of the water-color board with the black fabric paint.

5. When dry, spray the front and back of the fused fabric and board with several coats of clear acrylic spray. Let the acrylic dry thoroughly before applying the next coat.

6. Use a rotary cutter to cut the board into desired shapes. For the cat earrings, a 1-inch (2.5 cm) square was cut in half to make triangles while strips were cut for the frame.

7. Attach the contact-sheet print to a square of watercolor board with the fabric glue.

8. Glue the triangles to the top and bottom of the contact-print square, then glue the strips to create the frame.

9. Decorate the earrings with dots of dimensional "puffy" fabric paints.

10. Drill holes in the top of each earring, and attach the ear wires

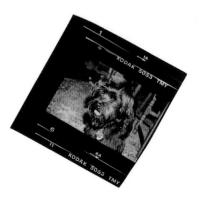

DESIGNER:
Peggy DeBell

Fused Fabric—Fun!

Turn any scrap of colorful fabric into a dynamic, dramatic, daring pair of earrings. Add a little paint, glue on some "jewels" or beads or buttons (or bows!), and you can have unlimited earrings to match every outfit.

MATERIALS

- Cotton fabric scraps
- Fabric paint
- Iron-on fusible web (used for fusing (bonding) fabric)
- Watercolor board, medium weight
- Clear acrylic spray
- Fabric glue
- Dimensional "puffy" fabric paints in colors of your choice
- Jump rings
- French ear wires

TOOLS

- Scissors
- Iron
- Artist's paintbrush
- Rotary fabric cutter
- Small hand drill or small motorized craft drill

INSTRUCTIONS

1. Take fabric scraps and iron them to remove any wrinkles.

2. Using the iron and fusible web, fuse the fabric to the water-color board following the manufacturer's instructions.

3. Paint the back of the water-color board with fabric paint in a color that coordinates with the fabric. Silver, copper, and gold paint can also be used and will give the backs a metallic look.

4. When the paint dries, spray the front and back of the fused fabric and paper with several coats of clear acrylic spray. Let the acrylic dry thoroughly before applying the next coat.

5. Using a rotary cutter, cut the board into a variety of shapes. It's helpful to sketch your ideas before beginning so you will have an idea of the shapes you'll need.

6. Following your design, glue the shapes together where you want them glued. You can give your earrings extra length and movement by attaching shapes with jump rings. Drill a small hole at the top of the shape you wish to attach, then drill a small hole at the bottom of the shape you will use for attaching it. Join the two shapes by inserting a jump ring through both holes.

7. Decorate the shapes with dimensional "puffy" fabric paint. Small dabs create beaded highlights.

8. Glue beads, buttons, or other decorative findings to the shapes.

9. Drill a small hole at the top of each earring and attach the ear wires.

DESIGNER:
Sandy Webster

Collage

You can create miniature works of wearable art in no time. (And if you don't tell, no one will know how simple they are to make.) If you enjoy working with scissors, paper, and glue, you have all the necessary skills to make these stunning collages.

MATERIALS

- Small sheet of cold-press water-color paper, 300# weight
- Various thin papers, cut and torn
- Acrylic medium—available in art- and craft-supply stores
- Watercolor paints
- Spray acrylic finish in gloss or matte
- Ear posts or findings
- Strong glue

TOOLS

- Scissors
- Small artist's brush

INSTRUCTIONS

1. Make a collage by first placing the cut and torn papers on the watercolor paper, arranging them in a design or pattern of your choice. Keep in mind the size of your earrings and work in proportion to that scale.

2. Using the brush and acrylic medium, paste the cut and torn paper to the watercolor paper. You don't need to apply the acrylic medium only to the back side of the pieces you're gluing. With this technique you can brush the cut and torn paper on the top or the back to fix it to the watercolor paper.

3. Use your watercolors to shade in areas. Let dry.

4. Cut out your earrings from this collage and watercolor the edges. Let dry.

5. With the acrylic medium, glue decorative or solid-color papers to the backs of the earrings. Or, you can watercolor the backs. Let dry.

6. Coat both the fronts and backs of the earrings with several more thin layers of acrylic medium, allowing the medium to dry between each coat.

7. When completely dry, spray with the acrylic finish of your choice.

8. Glue posts or clips to the back.

Variations

1. Consider adding thin, tiny pieces of fabric to the collage of papers.

2. Try collaging smaller pieces of collaged papers to the surface of the earring to give more dimension.

3. Beads and small found objects can be wired to the earrings before finishing the backs. Use a needle to make two small holes for threading the wire. Insert the wire from the back. Attach your beads or objects, then thread the wire through the front to the back. Twist both ends of the wire together, then finish the back.

4. For hanging earrings, take a small piece of thin jewelry wire and thread it through the bottom loop of an ear wire. Bend the wire in half over the loop, creating two ends. Using both ends as one, thread a bead onto the wire. Make sure the wire is long enough so that, when you are finished threading the bead, you have at least 1/4 inch (.5 cm) of wire extending from the bead. Glue one end of the wire to the front and one to the back of the earring. Using the collage technique, cover the wires with more papers, let dry, then finish with the acrylic spray.

Mosaics

Catch the light while capturing the look of stained glass with these colorful machine-embroidered mosaics. You'll get the same transparent color and diffused tones as you do with glass at a fraction of the weight. When you wear them, you should feel a certain serene sparkle.

These supplies will make several pairs of earrings, depending on the size you choose to make.

MATERIALS

- 12 inches (30.5 cm) of clear plastic yardage, medium weight—You can find this in general-merchandise stores; it is the same kind that is sold for tablecloths.
- Bits and pieces of metallic paper and metallic novelty fabric
- Paper towels
- Sewing thread in colors that match or harmonize with the metallics
- Small piece of cardboard for patterns
- White glue
- Dimensional "puffy" paint in iridescent colors
- Four or five clip clothespins
- Jump rings
- Earring findings of your choice

TOOLS

- Scissors
- Iron
- Sewing machine
- Paper punch
- Needle-nose pliers

INSTRUCTIONS

You will have the most success with this project if you have a basic knowledge of free machine embroidery. To do this, drop the teeth (feed dogs) on your sewing machine and remove the presser foot. Use a spring needle. (Watch your fingers as you sew!) You can also use a spring-shank embroidery foot with a regular needle. Set your machine for straight stitch. Don't worry about stitch length, it isn't important for this technique.

I. Cut two 10-inch (25.5 cm) squares of plastic. Place one flat on a table and arrange small pieces of metallic papers and fabrics in a mosaic-like pattern on the plastic. Remember to keep the size of the pieces in scale with the size of the earrings. Leave some clear areas here and there. Continue until you cover the square with an interesting arrangement of color and pattern.

2. When you are pleased with the arrangement, cover this layout with the other piece of plastic.

3. Cover both pieces with a piece of paper toweling. Gently press with a medium-heat, dry iron. This temporarily fuses the two pieces of plastic with the fabrics between.

4. Thread the sewing machine with coordinating thread and prepare it for free machine embroidery (see above). Stitch your "sandwich" of mosaics in a random, doodling motion. Move the stitching back, forth, and around, forming lines of stitching that will break the area into interesting small shapes and patterns. As you work, be sure to catch the small bits of fabric and color with the stitch to secure them to the layers of plastic.

5. When the stitching is completed to your satisfaction, make your pattern. Take the cardboard and cut a simple geometric shape that will be the exact size and shape of your earring. Mark one side A and the other side B.

6. Lay side A face up on the stitched plastic. Carefully cut around the pattern. Flip the pattern so side B is face up and cut another shape out of the plastic. This will give you a pair that is a mirror image. You can cut shapes that are exactly the same, or you can cut shapes that are different but harmonious in shape for a more interesting pair of earrings.

7. Run a thin line of white glue along the edges of each earring, securing the two layers of plastic and "locking" the stitching threads. Use clip clothespins to hold in place until the glue dries. Add a few dots of dimensional paint for "jewels" if you choose.

8. With a paper punch, punch a hole at the top of each earring, approximately ⅛ inch (.3 cm) from the edge. Insert a jump ring and ear wire or finding of your choice. Wear your earrings with joy—and make more to delight your friends!

complete circle

Just before her inauguration in 1953, Queen Elizabeth II of England pierced her ears. As a testament to this sovereign's popularity, a fervor of ear piercing swept the country. Pierced earring production in England rose 400 percent that year.

In the early 1960s, it became fashionable among college students to pierce their ears. Younger girls immediately followed their lead. A generation of mothers who had converted to clips watched as their modern daughters reverted to this age-old practice.

Nowadays it's not uncommon for mothers and even grandmothers to have a pierced lobe as well as multiple piercings on the ear's helix to accommodate several earrings.

GILDING

applying metallic leaf

Adding a bit of metallic leaf to your earrings will give them extra sparkle. You can find leaf in silver, gold, copper, and variegated colors at craft or art-supply shops.

To fix your leaf to the surface, you need to use a special adhesive known as "size." You apply the liquid size with a brush then wait until it dries partially and becomes "tacky," slightly sticky to the touch.

Handling metallic leaf can be tricky because it is so thin. It comes in packages of 25 sheets with each sheet of leaf separated by a piece of tissue paper. Handle your leaf with the tissue paper, using it to pick up and lay the leaf. When you need to tear or cut leaf, place the leaf between two pieces of the tissue paper, then proceed to tear or cut. This will give you some

extra thickness to work with, preventing damage to the delicate leaf.

Real gold leaf does not have to be sealed since it will not tarnish. If you are using composition gold leaf (made of brass containing zinc and copper) or copper leaf, you will have to apply a sealer coat to prevent the leaf from darkening over time. You can find sealer specifically for use on metallic leaf, or you can use a spray sealer preparation suitable for general art work.

DESIGNER:
Pei-Ling Becker

Longevity Earrings

To create a special gift for someone, incorporate symbolic objects or words into your design. Artist Pei-Ling Becker, a native of Taiwan, uses oriental symbolism to add a deeper meaning to the images she produces. While the design alone is visually attractive, the thoughts behind it give the earrings personal significance.

MATERIALS

- Mat board
- White glue
- Glitter
- Decorative rice paper
- Beads
- Cork
- Earring posts, or findings of your choice
- Strong glue or adhesive
- Gloss acrylic spray

TOOLS

- Craft knife or single-edge razor blade
- Artist's brush
- Scissors

INSTRUCTIONS

1. Using the craft knife or razor blade, carefully cut the mat board to the desired size and shape for background.

2. Brush a thin layer of white glue onto the mat board. Sprinkle glitter sparingly over the glue. The glitter will provide a nice background while the white glue provides a protective sealer coat for the mat board.

3. Cut the decorative paper into desired shapes.

4. Glue the paper, cork, beads, and other decorations to the mat board.

5. Attach posts or findings of your choice to the back of the earrings.

6. If you desire a shiny effect, a glossy spray acrylic coating may be applied.

DESIGNER:
Theresa Guthrie

Woven Fiber Earrings

You won't find these fabrics in any shop! With a large wooden bead as the form, you use needle and thread to create your own unique textiles for these woven earrings. The possibilities are endless when you discover how to add beads for sparkle and fringe for flair.

MATERIALS

- ½-inch (1.5 cm) or ¾-inch (2 cm) oval wooden beads
- Perle cotton thread, size 3
- Eye pins or head pins
- Yarns for weaving (also ribbons, metallic threads, or fibers)
- Seed beads or other beads for fringe and embellishments
- Disc beads
- Thread, size B
- Ear wires or posts

TOOLS

- Scissors
- Tapestry needle, #24
- Beading needle
- Wire cutters
- Round-nose pliers

INSTRUCTIONS

1. Thread approximately 48 inches (122 cm) of size 3 pearl cotton onto the tapestry needle. Double it.

2. Bring the needle and thread through the bead and tie it onto the bead as in Figure 1.

3. Hide the knot inside the bead and continue to wrap the thread in "spokes" around thread until you have 13 spokes. Wrap snugly. Using an odd number of spokes allows you to spiral endlessly around the bead as you weave (see Figure 2).

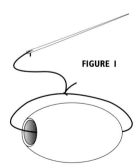

FIGURE 1

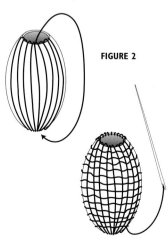

FIGURE 2

4. Fasten off the thread with a knot that is close to an end of the bead.

5. Thread the tapestry needle with about 24 inches (61 cm) of your weaving thread. Knot the end and pass the needle and thread through the center of the bead, catching the knot on an inside thread to secure it.

6. Start weaving at the top, going over then under each spoke. Do not push the rows too tightly together as you will lose the basket-weave effect. Continue weaving until the bead is covered. To end, thread the weaving thread under the last few rows and snip off.

7. For fringed earrings, use the size B thread, beading needle, and seed beads or beads of your choice to make fringes in the eye of the eye pin as in Figure 3.

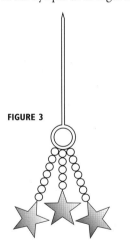

FIGURE 3

8. Thread the fringed eye pin through a disk bead and then through the woven wooden bead. Trim the eye pin to the desired length. Use round-nose pliers to form a loop for hanging an ear wire or post.

9. For the unfringed earrings, take a head pin and thread a smaller complementary bead on it, then a disk bead. Thread the head pin through the woven wooden bead. Thread another disk bead and a smaller bead on the head pin. Trim the head pin with the wire cutters leaving enough to make a loop. Using the round-nose pliers, form a loop for securing the ear wire or post.

TIPS:

Experiment with different threads, ribbons, or fibers as your weaving thread. Try using more than one color or metallic thread for your weaving. Embellish the earrings with seed beads or other beads by sewing them on with matching thread. Start your project on a round wooden bead or even a spool-shaped one.

in the beginning

It is thought that the earliest humans pierced the lobes of their ears to mark initiation ceremonies. Objects were inserted to keep the holes from closing during the natural healing process so the scar of the piercing would remain as an indelible, outward sign of an individual's status within a community. At some point people realized an object could remain in the pierced lobe while the hole healed around the object.

Because it's believed that many of the earliest earrings were fashioned out of perishable materials, there is no way of knowing exactly what people used as the first earrings. These ornaments might have been a shell, a piece of wood, a bundle of reeds or needles, a shiny stone, or an animal bone.

DESIGNER:
Leigh McAdams

Block-Printed Beads

Once you learn how to make these paper beads, you'll be able to come up with almost endless designs and color schemes for every occasion. They're striking enough to take center stage, or harmonize them with complementary beads.

MATERIALS

- Corrugated cardboard
- White glue
- Polystyrene trays—optional (the trays used for packaging meat or fruit)
- Heavy drawing paper, 12 x 18 inches (30.5 x 45.5 cm)—60- or 70- pound paper works best
- Black acrylic paint
- Paper plates for mixing paint
- White or iridescent white acrylic paint
- 10 inches (25.5 cm) of stiff wire
- Clear spray lacquer or polyurethane
- 2 silver head pins
- 4, 8mm glass or stone beads
- 4, black 8° seed beads
- 2 silver ear wires

TOOLS

- Scissors
- Metal ruler
- Utility knife
- Foam brushes
- Pencil
- Wood dowel or metal rod, ⅛ inch (.3 cm) in diameter and 7 inches (19 cm) long
- Rag
- Wire cutters
- Round-nose pliers

INSTRUCTIONS

1. To make the block for printing, cut two pieces of corrugated cardboard, each 6 x 6 inches (15 x 15 cm). Glue the two pieces together using the white glue. Place a heavy book on the glued pieces while they dry.

2. Cut several strips of cardboard, ¼ inch (.5 cm) wide, by holding the metal ruler securely on the cardboard and running the utility knife close to the edge of the ruler to make a straight cut.

3. Glue these strips diagonally to one side of the glued cardboard pieces, leaving about ¼ inch (.5 cm) between each strip. Allow to dry thoroughly. The cardboard provides a nice texture for your print. If you prefer a smoother look, cut the strips from the polystyrene trays.

4. Using a 2- or 3-inch (5 or 7.5 cm) foam brush, paint the background color on the heavy drawing paper. Don't worry if the color looks uneven, this will add texture and interest to the finished beads. Allow the paint to dry.

5. Squeeze some white paint on a paper plate. (For an interesting look try iridescent paints.) Mix a small amount of water in the paint until it is of a smooth consistency a little thicker than cream.

6. With the foam brush, apply the white paint to the surface of the block with the diagonal strips. Press the block, painted side down, onto a piece of scrap paper, then recoat it with paint. Do this three or four times until you get a complete print.

7. Starting in the upper left corner of your painted paper, use the block to print, moving from left to right and covering the whole paper with the pattern. Let the paper dry completely.

8. Place the paper pattern side down. Use a ruler and pencil to draw straight cutting lines. For this project you will need to cut:
• two pieces 1¾ inch x 12 inches (4.5 x 30.5 cm);
• four pieces ½ inch x 12 inches (1.5 x 30.5 cm); and
• four pieces ⅜ inch x 12 inches (10 x 30.5 cm) as in Figure 1.

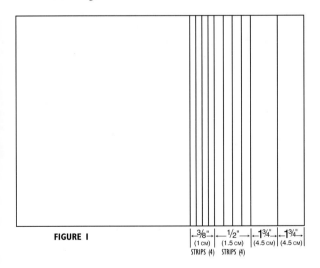

FIGURE I

⅜" (1 CM) STRIPS (4) | ½" (1.5 CM) STRIPS (4) | 1¾" (4.5 CM) | 1¾" (4.5 CM)

9. Take the dowel or rod and begin to roll one of the 1¾-inch (4.5 cm) pieces around it. Roll and unroll the end several times to start the curl, then begin rolling the paper around the rod as tightly as possible. Try to keep the roll as even as possible. When you get within 1½ inch (4 cm) of the end, stop and apply the glue on the last 1 inch (2.5 cm) of paper as in Figure 2.

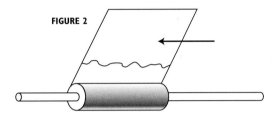

FIGURE 2

10. Wipe off any excess glue with your finger, using a damp rag to wipe your fingers as needed to prevent them from sticking to the paper. Roll the other 1¾-inch (4.5 cm) piece in the same manner.

11. Position one of the ½-inch (1.5 cm) pieces on the lower half of one of the two cylinders you've just made so that it is ½ inch (1.5 cm) from the end of the cylinder as in Figure 3. Roll as tightly as possible. Place the other ½-inch (1.5 cm) piece on the top half of the cylinder ½ inch (1.5 cm) from the edge and roll as above.

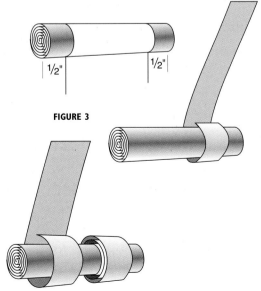

½" ½"

FIGURE 3

12. Roll the ⅜-inch (1 cm) rectangles on top of the ½-inch (1.5 cm) cylinders as in Figure 4. Make another so you have two "beads." Let the glue dry, then string the beads on stiff wire. Hang them in an area with good ventilation and spray them with two or three coats of clear lacquer or polyurethane. Allow each coat to dry thoroughly before applying the next one.

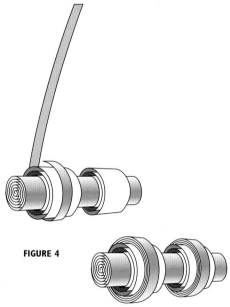

FIGURE 4

Variations

Different sizes and shapes of beads can be made by cutting different shapes from the decorated paper. The elongated ovals were made by cutting a long narrow triangle, 2 inches (5 cm) at the base and ¼ inch (.5 cm) at the tip as in Figure 5.

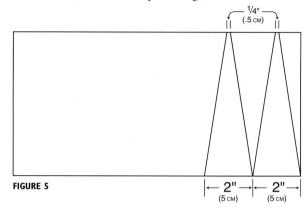

FIGURE 5

13. To assemble your earrings, take a head pin and string on one seed bead, one 8mm bead, the paper cylinder, one 8mm bead and finally one seed bead. Cut off the excess wire of the head pin, leaving at least ¼ inch (.5 cm) to ⅜ inch (1 cm) for the loop. With the round-nose pliers, make a loop, insert an ear wire, then close the loop.

METAL

When you think of working with metal, do you conjure up images of bubbling acid baths and hot torches? Don't let these thoughts stop you. With just pliers, some cutters, your hands, and a few feet (centimeters) of wire or a small square of sheet metal you can create stunning earrings that are easy to make while giving you the irreplaceable look of handcrafted metal.

MELANIE ALTER
Copper, Gold, and Brass

Tools

ROUND-NOSE, FLAT-NOSE, NEEDLE-NOSE, and chain-nose pliers will help you when working with metal. You can easily find good pliers at craft shops or hardware stores. For making earrings, look for small pliers that are suitable for craft work.

Round-nose pliers are essential. They enable you to make smooth curves and provide a rounded surface for wrapping wire or sheet metal into graceful shapes. Flat-nose pliers have wider, more substantial jaws that are good for gripping or holding metal firmly. Flat-nose pliers also provide a good edge for bending sharp angles. Needle-nose pliers have long slender jaws, useful for delicate work. Chain-nose pliers have tapered jaws with rounded exteriors that are helpful for working in small spaces.

You will get the best results from using smooth-jawed pliers. Pliers with serrated jaws will mar the metal. You can tape the jaws of serrated pliers or use an adhesive bandage, padded-side up, on the inner surface of the jaws. However, for the minimal extra cost, smooth-jawed pliers are superior for this work.

DIAGONAL CUTTERS, with their pointed tips, help you get into tight places, making a clean cut. Again, choose small cutters suitable for craft work. For working with sheet metal, you will need tin snips or metal sheers.

A JIG is a guide for bending wire into a predetermined shape. By bending the wire in a repeating pattern on a jig, you can create units that are the same size and shape. You can make your own jig with scrap wood and nails. Sturdy commercially made jigs are available at craft stores, in bead- lapidary- or jewelry-supply shops, or through jewelry-supply catalogs.

Some people enjoy working almost exclusively with a jig, others find free-form work to be the most satisfying. It's fun to try both, then see what you think.

A JEWELER'S SAW has interchangeable blades, from extra fine to coarse, depending on the work you're doing. If you don't have a jeweler's saw, you can use a jigsaw with a fine blade suitable for metal. (Lisa Randall provides some tips for sawing on page 101.)

FILES enable you to remove burrs, those ragged pieces of metal created by cutting. You can get small files at craft or hardware stores. If you need to buy a file, a good all-purpose jewelry file is an equalling file, 4-cut.

VISES can be helpful for holding the end of wire or sheet stock when you work. A hand-held pin vise is specially designed to hold the end of wire and is used for wrapping projects. C-clamps also come in handy and can act as a makeshift vise.

BETTY BACON
Gold and Crystal Ear Cuffs

Wire and Sheet Metal

Copper, brass, base metal, silver, gold, gold-filled… where to begin? If you're just starting out, let price determine the metals you'll use. Gold, gold-filled, and silver are much more expensive than copper, brass, and base metal. Practice with them first, then when you've perfected your technique, use the more expensive materials.

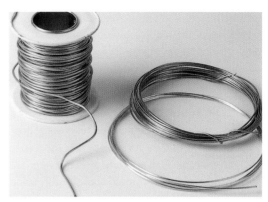

WIRE is an incredibly versatile material for working with earrings. You can wrap it around lapidary, string beads on it, bend it, coil it, and wrap it into exquisite shapes all by itself. (Kate Drew-Wilkinson provides an artistic example of a wrapped wire design for suspending beads or charms on page 87.)

By "drawing" metal through successively smaller holes in a "draw plate," wire can be made in varying diameters. A standardized measurement of the diameter of wire is known as the "gauge." The lower the number of the gauge, the thicker the wire; 14-gauge is thicker than 23-gauge for instance. Lower-gauge wire (thicker) is slightly more difficult to work than higher-gauge wire because of the increased diameter which naturally makes it stiffer.

Wire can be round, half-round, square, oval, or triangular in shape. It comes in copper, brass, sterling silver, gold-filled (a layer of gold fused to base metal), gold, or in anodized niobium, titanium, and aluminum. Anodizing is a process of coloring metal by first submerging it in a chemical bath, then passing an electric current through the chemicals which imparts a film of color to the surface of the metal.

You can find wire at hardware stores, in craft shops, bead stores or shops specializing in lapidary or jewelry supplies. You can also buy direct from jewelry-supply catalogs. If you are just starting out with wire, work with copper and brass wire first before working with the more costly silver, gold, and anodized metals.

To make wire easier to work it is "annealed." To do this, the wire is heated, then cooled. Most wire you buy for craft work has already been annealed. If you don't know whether this has been done, test it out. Bend the wire with your fingers. If it bends easily, it probably has been annealed.

A WORD OF CAUTION. If you have pierced ears, do not use copper or brass for ear wires or posts. Some people are sensitive to these metals and they may cause allergic reactions when inserted into a piercing. It is better to use commercial wires and posts that are made of hypo-allergenic metal. If you do make your own wires or posts, they should be made of silver, gold, or gold-filled wire. When using commercial ear findings, the large variety available will allow you to find a safe metal in a finish to coordinate with the metal you're using in your project.

SHEET METAL is made by passing the metal thorough a series of heavy rollers that are set to create successively thinner sheets. Like wire, sheet metal comes in different gauges that indicate its thickness—the higher the number of gauge, the thinner the sheet. You can buy sheet metal in shops that carry jewelry-making supplies, including some bead and lapidary shops, or through jewelry-supply catalogs.

Again, if you are just starting out with sheet metal, experiment with the less expensive metals such as brass and copper before moving on to sterling silver, gold-filed, or gold.

Finishes

When copper, silver, and brass are exposed to air, they undergo a natural process known as oxidation. Oxidation will turn metal dark over time. With the right conditions and on certain metals, it leads to rust. To control natural oxidation you can polish the metal or apply a finish.

JEWELER'S ROUGE, a fine abrasive used for polishing the surface of the metal, is commonly used for evening out the small nicks and dents you might make when using pliers on metal.

It comes in a cake or in a can, and you can find it at bead shops, lapidary shops, or through jewelry-supply catalogs. You can also use commercial polishing cloths. Polishing with jeweler's rouge or cloths will not prevent oxidation. For metal that has not been sealed, you will need to polish it occasionally to maintain the shine.

LACQUER provides a barrier between the metal and the air, preventing any further oxidation (darkening) of the metal. You can purchase special jeweler's lacquer or use a high-grade, non-yellowing commercial lacquer. Carefully dip the pieces in lacquer, hanging them to dry and allowing them to dry thoroughly. Humidity levels will affect the drying time, so be patient.

NEVER LACQUER SILVER. Over time, lacquer on silver turns yellow and makes the silver look as if it's been dipped in glue. It's better to polish the silver occasionally to control the oxidation.

JACALYN BRULL
Sterling silver

KATE DREW-WILKINSON
*Beautiful wire wrapping for
suspending a special bead or charm*

ANTIQUING METAL can be accomplished with commercial preparations. Some of these products may be toxic, so follow the manufacturer's precautions when using them.

LIVER OF SULPHUR is a simple way to antique metal and is available where you buy jewelry supplies. Liver of sulphur, when dissolved in water, creates a solution that speeds the natural oxidation process of metal. The liquid will turn the metal black, creating an "oxidized" finish (see page 93).

You control how much or how little of the finish you want by using pumice to remove the oxidation. A good, readily available pumice is nonchlorine abrasive cleanser which you can find in grocery stores. When you are satisfied with the amount of oxidation, seal the metal (excepting silver) with lacquer to prevent any further natural oxidation.

communication, status, and the art of flirting

While the act itself of piercing the lobe may not retain much significance in modern society, we continue to wear earrings for many of the same reasons as our primitive ancestors. Like other adornments, earrings can be thought of as a form of communication, a way of announcing our status in society. We choose our earrings to subtly tell others who we are, what we believe, our economic standing, artistic tastes, or sentimental leanings.

We often wear earrings as a means of flirtation. After all, earrings are worn on the earlobe, an acknowledged erogenous zone. Their close proximity to the face sets earrings apart from most other jewelry. Who hasn't carefully chosen earrings on occasion to purposefully draw attention to themselves in the hopes of engaging another in meaningful gaze?

DESIGNER:
Ellsworth "Ed" Sinclair

Ornamental Earrings

The shimmer of gold and silver reflects the color of the crystal beads in these elegant earrings. Their classic look captures the feeling of romantic, candlelit evenings or a festive New Year's Eve.

MATERIALS
(FOR ONE PAIR)

- 45 inches (114.5 cm) of 22-gauge, 14kt. gold-filled square wire, half hard
- 128, 2mm drilled, sterling silver beads
- 4, 2mm drilled, gold-filled beads
- 12, 4mm diamond-shaped, drilled, Swarovski beads (crystal)
- 2 ear wires

TOOLS

- Ruler
- 4-inch (10 cm) side cutters
- Pin vise (small hand-held vise used for wrapping wire, available at craft stores, jewelry-supply and lapidary-supply shops)
- Small bench vise
- 4-inch (10 cm) chain-nose pliers
- 4-inch (10 cm) flat-nose pliers
- 4-inch (10 cm) round-nose pliers

(All pliers and cutter above are a standard set of wirewrap tools.)

INSTRUCTIONS

1. For each earring, cut: three wires 4 inches (10 cm) long; one wire 6 inches (15 cm) long; and one wire 3 inches (7.5 cm) long. Clean and straighten the wire.

2. Bend one end of each of the 6-inch (15 cm) wires, ½ inch (1.5 cm) from the ends as in Figure 1A and 1B.

FIGURE 1A

FIGURE 1B

3. Put the three 4-inch (10 cm) wires together. Take one of the 6-inch (15 cm) wires and, beginning at the center, *wrap it tightly* three times around the 4-inch (10 cm) wires. When you finish wrapping three times, the ends of the 6-inch (15 cm) wire should be opposite one another as shown in Figure 2. Trim only the shorter end of the 6-inch (15 cm) wire, leaving the other end long. This long end will become the center post and platform for the earring.

FIGURE 2

4. Bend the longer part of the 6-inch (15 cm) wrap wire up so it is perpendicular to the flat surface of the group of 4-inch (10 cm) wires as in Figure 3.

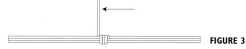

FIGURE 3

5. Spread the three 4-inch (10 cm) wires apart as in Figure 4.

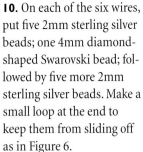

FIGURE 4

6. Using the pin vise, twist each of the wires separately, including the center post wire. A fine (tight) twist is recommended.

7. After all the wires have been twisted, measure ¾ inch (2 cm) up the center post and bend as indicated in Figures 5A and 5B.

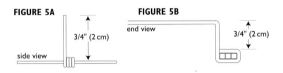

FIGURE 5A

3/4" (2 cm)

side view

FIGURE 5B

end view

3/4" (2 cm)

8. Bend this ¾-inch (2 cm) length around the perpendicular post (Figure 5C), rolling it until it is a flat disk as in Figures 5D and 5E.

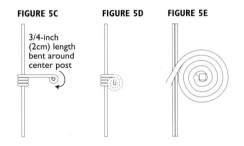

FIGURE 5C

3/4-inch (2cm) length bent around center post

FIGURE 5D

FIGURE 5E

9. Bend the three wires to cover the wrap wire so that the center post is perpendicualr to the three wires. The other

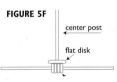

FIGURE 5F

center post

flat disk

ends of the wrap wire will cover the center post platform. When finished it will look like Figure 5F.

10. On each of the six wires, put five 2mm sterling silver beads; one 4mm diamond-shaped Swarovski bead; followed by five more 2mm sterling silver beads. Make a small loop at the end to keep them from sliding off as in Figure 6.

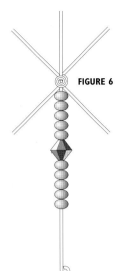

FIGURE 6

11. Once you have put the beads on each of the six wires, string the beads on the center post. Begin with two 2mm sterling silver beads; two 2mm gold-filled beads; then two more 2mm sterling silver beads as shown in Figure 7. Make a small loop at the end of the center post.

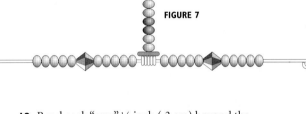

FIGURE 7

12. Bend each "arm" ⅛ inch (.3 cm) beyond the last bead as shown in Figure 8.

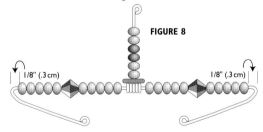

FIGURE 8

1/8" (.3 cm)

1/8" (.3 cm)

13. *Gently bend all six "arms" as shown in Figure 9.*

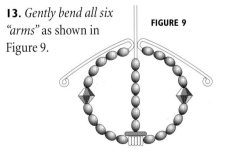

FIGURE 9

14. Place one end of the 3-inch (7.5 cm) piece of wire in the bench vise. Grasp the other end with the pin vise and make a fine (tight) twist. When you have completed the twist, grasp the end that was in the pin vise with the flat-nose pliers. Use the flat-nose pliers to pull the wire into a small circle as shown in Figure 10.

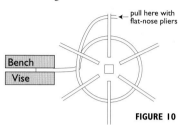

pull here with
flat-nose pliers

Bench
Vise

FIGURE 10

15. Keep the circle in the bench vise and insert all six of the bent-over arms into the circle. Make sure the center post is in the center of the circle. Using the flat-nose pliers, pull the circle until it is closed, making sure all six of the bent-over arms are distributed evenly around the center post. Continue to pull the circle until it is *very, very snug* around the arms as in Figure 10.

16. Remove the assembly from the vise, and continue to wrap the wire tightly for two full turns around the center post. Cut off the excess wire and tuck the ends into the coil created by the two turns.

17. Make sure each wire arm (those radiating from the center post) is bent away from the center post and is directly over the row of 2mm beads on its other end. The looped ends are now made into flat discs around the center post. (Refer to the photo of the finished earrings).

18. The center post can be cut short or left long. Whatever length you choose, make sure to leave enough wire to make a loop for attaching the ear wires.

19. Attach the ear wires.

DESIGNER:
Jacalyn Brull

Cone Earrings

The natural cone shape and meandering spirals of these earrings suggest morning glories climbing a fence. It's hard to believe that the graceful curves and loops of this design were once sheet metal and wire. Make them in their shorter version, or use a little extra wire for more length and added swing.

MATERIALS

- 2¼ x 2½-inch (5.5 cm x 6.5 cm) piece of 30-gauge sheet metal (you can use silver, gold-filled, or copper)
- 13 inches (33 cm) of 10-gauge half-round sterling silver wire.
- French wires

TOOLS

- Metal shears or tin snips
- Fine-cut file (use only a fine file, a coarse file will tear the metal)
- Round-nose pliers
- Sandpaper in 600 grit

OPTIONAL:

- Mallet
- Liver of sulphur (for patina finish)
- Disposable plastic container
- Polishing cloth

INSTRUCTIONS

1. Using the metal shears or tin snips, cut two rectangles, each 1⅛ x 1¼ inch (2.8 x 3 cm) out of the 30-gauge metal.

2. If the rectangles curled when you cut them, lay them on a flat surface and gently tap them with the mallet to flatten them.

3. File the edges smooth and file the corners round.

4. Using the 600-grit sandpaper, sand the edges.

5. Lay the rectangle on a flat surface and hold it down while you sand the surface using the 600-grit sandpaper. Be sure to sand in one direction rather than back and forth. This will give you a smooth, one-way grain.

6. Turn the rectangle over so the sanded side is now face down.

7. With the round-nose pliers, grasp the bottom right-hand corner of the rectangle between the jaws of the pliers. When you are making the opposite earring, you want to start in the lower left-hand corner.

8. Begin rolling the rectangle in a diagonal direction towards the opposite corner. For one earring you will be rolling toward the upper left-hand corner, for the other earring you will be rolling toward the upper right-hand corner. Make one complete turn over one jaw of the pliers.

9. After making one complete turn, pull the pliers out and slip the opposite jaw of the pliers into that same turn as in Figure 1.

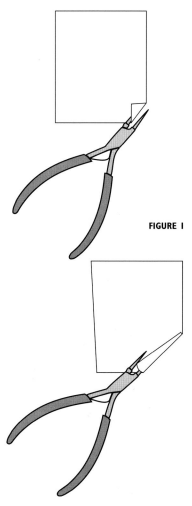

FIGURE I

10. Roll the metal over both jaws of the pliers until you've rolled all but the left corner (the right corner for the opposite earring). This will give you a cone shape. Make sure you do not roll the metal too tightly. You want enough room in the center of the narrowest part of the cone (the bottom) to allow for threading a 10-gauge wire. Remove the pliers.

11. Take the pliers and roll the top corner in the opposite direction, bending the top tip slightly down as in Figure 2.

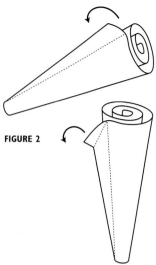

FIGURE 2

12. If you have wound the metal too tightly and cannot fit the 10-gauge wire through the cone, place the tip of the pliers into the narrow end (the bottom) of the cone and wiggle it around to stretch the opening.

13. Cut two 4½-inch (11.5 cm) pieces of 10-gauge half-round wire.

14. File, then sand both ends of the wire. You can file the ends flat, but you will get a nicer effect if you slightly taper both ends of the wire as you file.

15. Thread the 10-gauge wire through the cone. Leave a ½-inch (1.5 cm) to ¾-inch (2 cm) tail extending from the bottom of the cone (see Figure 3A).

FIGURE 3A

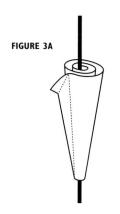

16. Using the round-nose pliers, grasp the end of the tail extending from the bottom of the cone and tightly curl the wire as in Figure 3B.

FIGURE 3B

17. Using your fingers, bend the wire that extends from the top of the cone. You don't want a sharp angle but more of a gentle loop (see Figure 4A).

FIGURE 4A

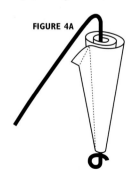

18. Wrap the remaining wire around the cone with your fingers as in Figure 4B. It will help if you hold the top loop with one hand and wrap with the other.

FIGURE 4B

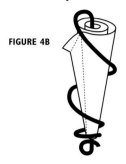

19. When you get to the bottom of the cone, you should have a short length of 10-gauge wire remaining. Use the pliers to wrap this around the curl that extends from the bottom of the cone.

20. You can stop at this point and attach the French wires at the loop at the top of the cone. However, if you want additional length and more movement to the earrings, you will have to add another piece. The next five steps will tell you how to do this.

Adding Length and Movement

YOU WILL NEED:

- 2, 2-inch (5 cm) pieces of 10-gauge half-round wire

INSTRUCTIONS

1. File both ends of the wire. You can file the ends flat but will get a nicer effect if you slightly taper the ends as you file.

2. With its flat side up, slip one of the 2-inch (5 cm) pieces through the loop at the top of the cone. Position the wire so that approximately ⅜ inch (1 cm) extends beyond the loop at the top of the cone. This short piece will become the loop that encircles the loop at the top of the cone.

3. Using the pliers, grasp the left end of the ⅜-inch (1 cm) piece of wire and roll it into a loop over the loop at the top of the cone as in Figure 5. (For the opposite earring, you'll grasp the right end of the wire.)

FIGURE 5

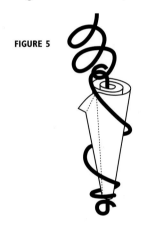

4. Using your hands or pliers, create loops with the remaining wire. You can make loops that are uniform in shape or ones that are more free-form. Just be sure to leave enough wire at the end to curl into one complete loop for attaching the ear wire.

5. Curl the end into a loop and attach the French wire. Repeat these steps for the other earring.

Creating a Patina Finish

A patina finish (also called an oxidized or antiqued finish) will give depth to the earrings by creating highlights and shadows that will enhance the look of the silver. The liver of sulphur turns the metal dark. You control the amount of finish by removing as much or as little of the color as you want with the polishing cloth.

YOU WILL NEED:

• Liver of sulphur

• Disposable plastic container

• Clean stick

• Polishing cloth

INSTRUCTIONS

I. Take a piece of liver of sulphur the size of a pea and place it in a plastic container. You want a container you can throw away after you are finished.

2. Add very hot tap water and stir with a nonmetallic object such as a paint stirrer or clean stick.

3. Drop the earrings into the solution and watch as they darken.

4. Remove the earrings from the solution. Run them under cold water to rinse. Dry them with a clean cloth.

5. Polish the earrings with the polishing cloth. This should leave the earrings with a toned-down, "mellow" finish.

it can be done

In some parts of the world it is considered a status symbol for women to have elongated, stretched earlobes that can accommodate many heavy hoops of gold and silver. Beginning in early childhood, the earlobes are progressively enlarged with ear plugs of increasing diameter. Eventually large hoops are hung from the lobes. Over time, as more hoops are added, a woman's earlobes can reach her shoulders.

DESIGNER:
Betty Bacon

Follow That Curve

Watch out! Making bent-wire jewelry will lead you through some interesting twists and turns. Once you discover you can make almost infinite designs from this versatile material, you'll be hooked. This design was made on a jig, a tool that gives you a fun and easy way to shape wire.

MATERIALS

- 12 inches (30.5 cm) of 16-gauge round sterling silver wire
- 2 silver ear wires

TOOLS

- Wire cutters
- Round-nose pliers
- 1-inch (2.5 cm) WigJig, a commercial jig available at bead shops and craft stores

INSTRUCTIONS

1. Cut 5 inches (12.5 cm) of 16-gauge wire. After you cut the wire, you'll notice it curves in one direction. You will have the most success with wire if you don't torture it but work with its natural tendencies. Follow the wire's curve, and using the round-nose pliers, make a loop at the end of the wire against that curve.

2. Following Figure 1, place the wire on peg 2, ⅜ inch (1 cm) from the loop. Bend the wire around loop 2.

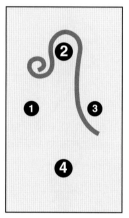

FIGURE 1

3. Continue down to the left of peg 3, then up and around peg 3 as in Figure 2.

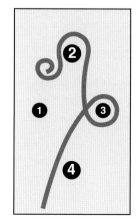

FIGURE 2

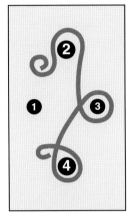

FIGURE 3

4. Bring the wire down to the left of peg 4, then make an oval loop around peg 4, as in Figure 3.

5. Continue past peg 4 and make another loop close to the oval loop.

6. Use your fingers to move the wire into the shape you desire. You can leave the loops as they are when they come off the jig, or you can gently press them closer together for a tighter look (see photos).

7. Cut 1 inch (2.5 cm) of the 16-gauge wire. Using the round nose pliers make a loop at one end. At the other end make a loop that is the reverse of the first loop. When you've finished both loops you should have a piece that resembles a figure eight.

8. Attach one of the loops of the figure eight to the top of the bent-wire earring. Attach one of the ear wires to the top loop of the figure eight.

jigs

A jig is any form used to guide wire into a predetermined shape. It's an essential tool when you want to produce identical pieces from one design. A jig is most helpful when you're making a piece of jewelry that's made up of many similar units. Using a jig will save you time and ensure that all the units you make will be uniform in size and shape.

Don't get the impression that jigs are strictly for making mass-produced jewelry. Jigs can be fun to use anytime and are great tools in helping you design bent-wire earrings.

You can make your own jigs using scrap wood and nails. But you might find a commercial jig, such as the WigJig, is more convenient and easier to use since they are sturdy tools crafted especially for repeated use.

A jig is a good way to teach yourself wire basics. Buy some copper or brass wire and let yourself play. Since copper and brass are much less expensive than silver or gold-filled wire, use them as your sketching materials. When you have a design you like, try fashioning it out of more expensive wire.

DESIGNER:
Betty Bacon

Ins and Outs

Working with wire is basically very simple. All you need is wires, pliers, and you. Making bent-wire jewelry requires no soldering, allowing you the freedom to take your work with you wherever you go.

Red Squares

MATERIALS

- 2, 2½-inch (6.5 cm) lengths of 20-gauge square sterling silver wire
- 2 square beads, one large and one small
- 2 silver ear wires

TOOLS

- Wire cutters
- Round-nose pliers
- Flat-nose pliers

INSTRUCTIONS

Note: When you're trying to make identical pieces such as earrings out of bent wire, you might find it easier to work in an assembly-line method—once you complete one step on one length, repeat that step on the other length. This will help you make the pieces more uniform in size and shape, giving you a matched pair.

1. Cut two lengths of 20-gauge wire, each 2½ inches (6.5 cm) long.

2. Hold one end of the wire with your fingers and grasp the other end with the flat-nose pliers. Lightly twist the wire. You don't want a tight twist, just a loose twist running the length of each wire to give it interest.

3. Using the round-nose pliers, make a small loop on one end of each length of wire.

4. Take one length and use the flat-nose pliers to make a sharp turn down (right angle) ⅛ inch (.3 cm) from the end of the loop you made in Step 3.

5. Make another right-angle turn back (like a hairpin turn), ⅛ inch (.3 cm) from the first turn.

6. Move the pliers ½ inch (1.5 cm) over from the turn you made in Step 5 and make a right angle downward.

7. Move the pliers ⅛ inch (.3 cm) down from the angle you made in Step 6 and make a right angle back (as in Step 5). Place a small bead on the wire.

8. Make another right angle downward.

9. Make a right-angle turn back, ½ inch (1.5 cm) down from the angle you made in Step 8. Place a large bead on the wire.

10. Make another turn up beside the beads. The end of the wire should now extend past the center of the small bead.

11. Make a final right-angle turn toward the small bead and cut the wire. Place the end of the wire inside the small bead.

12. Attach the ear wires to the loops at the top of the earrings.

Use your imagination to devise designs that incorporate special beads and you have an almost instant pair of earrings. If you're just beginning, practice your techniques on less expensive brass and copper wire before using silver wire.

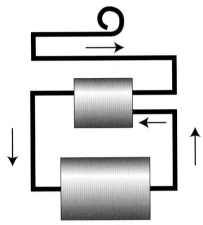

BENDING DIAGRAM FOR RED SQUARES EARRINGS

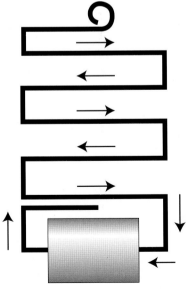

BENDING DIAGRAM FOR GREEN LADDER EARRINGS

Green Ladder

MATERIALS

- 2, 6-inch (15 cm) lengths of 20-gauge square sterling silver wire
- 2 modern glass beads

TOOLS

- Wire cutters
- Round-nose pliers
- Flat-nose pliers

INSTRUCTIONS

1. With the round-nose pliers, make a loop on the end of the wire, using ½ inch (1.5 cm) of the wire.

2. Bend the wire at ¼ inch (.5 cm).

3. Bend the wire at ½ inch (1.5 cm), then again at ¼ inch (.5 cm).

4. Alternate bending the wire at ¼ inch (.5 cm) with bending it at ½ inch (1.5 cm) until you have the length you want, minus the bead.

5. Place the bead on the wire and make the rectangle around it. Depending on the size of your bead, you may need to make the last rectangle larger to accommodate it. Overlap the wires above the bead.

6. Attach the ear wires to the loops at the top of the earrings.

DESIGNER:
Betty Bacon

Round and Round

*These two designs give you more ideas on how
you can bend wire for different effects.*

Swirled Wire with Rose Bead

MATERIALS

- 2, 10-inch (25.5 cm) lengths of 20-gauge square sterling silver wire
- 2 square modern glass beads
- 2 silver ear wires

TOOLS

- Wire cutters
- Round-nose pliers
- Flat-nose pliers

INSTRUCTIONS

1. Starting at the small end (the tip) of the flat-nose pliers, wrap the wire around the closed pliers five times.

2. Remove this spiral from the pliers. Don't cut the wire at this time.

3. Using the round-nose pliers, make a loop on the small end of the wire coil.

4. Place the bead on the wire at the large end of the coil, then bring the wire to the opposite side of the coil, making a large half circle.

5. Cut off the excess wire. Make a small loop at the end for attaching the end of the wire to the coil. Hook the loop to the bottom spiral of the coil.

6. With your fingers, press the coils into the shape you desire.

7. Attach the ear wires to the top loops of each earring.

Circle Loops with Striped Purple Beads

MATERIALS

- 2, 2½-inch (6.5 cm) lengths of 20-gauge square sterling silver wire
- 2 large silver jump rings
- 2 round purple beads
- 2 silver ear wires

TOOLS

- Wire cutters
- Round-nose pliers

INSTRUCTIONS

1. Using the round-nose pliers make a figure eight at the end of each length of wire. *Do not cut the wire!*

2. Use your fingers to loop the wire in a large circle and then back across the middle of the figure eight.

3. With your fingers, continue to make a gentle curve that goes down and around to the bottom of the large circle.

4. With the round-nose pliers, make a small loop at the end of the curve.

5. String the bead on the large jump ring. Attach the jump ring to the loop at the end of the curve.

6. Attach the ear wires to the top loops of each earring.

DESIGNER:
Jacalyn Brull

Squiggles

This free-form design is lighthearted and fun (and is easier to make than it looks). By combining beads or stones with sterling silver wire, you'll have a sparkling pair of earrings in no time.

MATERIALS

- 9 inches (23 cm) of 10- or 12-gauge half-round sterling silver wire
- 16 inches (40.5 cm) of 24-gauge round sterling silver wire
- 10–12 small beads (4 or 5 mm) or stone chip beads
- 2 French wires

TOOLS

- Wire cutters
- File
- Round-nose pliers

INSTRUCTIONS

1. Cut two pieces of the 10- or 12-gauge half-round wire, each 4½ inches (11.5 cm) long.

2. Using the file, file one end of each piece round and the other end flat.

3. Taking one of the pieces, use the round-nose pliers to grip the end of the wire that has been filed flat. Position the wire in the pliers so the flat side of the half-round wire is facing up. Curl the wire to form a loop.

4. Using the pliers, grip the wire under this first loop. Hold the remaining wire with your other hand. Begin bending the wire, looping it in opposite directions.

5. Bend the last bit of wire into a tight curl. *Note:* To make the loops more uniform, do one as your "learning" loop and try to repeat what you did on the other loops.

6. After forming the loops, use your fingers to pull the loops slightly apart, making sure the metal does not quite meet. This will give your piece more dimension. Repeat Steps 3–6 on the other half-round piece.

7. Cut two pieces of 24-gauge round wire, each 8 inches (20.5 cm) long.

8. Wrap one of the pieces of 24-gauge round wire three to four times around the top of one of the half-round wire pieces (under the top loop).

9. Thread a bead or stone chip through the 24-gauge wire until it touches the half-round piece.

10. While holding the bead or stone in place, wrap the 24-gauge round wire once around the half-round piece so that the bead or stone is secure.

11. Repeat Steps 9–10, (stringing, then wrapping) until you get to the bottom curl of the half-round piece.

12. Wrap the excess 24-gauge wire above the curl three or four times.

13. Cut off any excess wire.

14. To flatten the cut end, use the pliers to pinch the last wrapping against the half-round piece

15. Repeat Steps 8–14 on the other half-round wire piece

16. Attach the French wire findings to the top loop of the half-round pieces.

DESIGNER:
Lisa Randall

Sheer Joy

These happy, carefree figures will tirelessly leap through the rhythms of your day. Everyone you meet will smile at the sheer joy of life they express. Once you discover how easy they are to make, you'll be dancing too.

MATERIALS

- Sheet of 20-gauge sterling silver, copper, or brass (available at jewelry-supply shops)
- Jump rings
- French wires

TOOLS

- Scissors
- Rubber cement
- Jigsaw and fine saw blades
- Fine-cut file
- Sandpaper in 600 and 1000 grit
- Round-nose pliers

INSTRUCTIONS

1. Design a simple shape. Photo copy the design, enlarging or reducing it until you get it to the size you want for the earrings you will make.

2. Once you get the design to the right size, draw a tab ⅛ inch (.3 cm) wide and ¼ inch (.5 cm) long extending from the top of the design. This will become the guide for cutting the loop that is used for attaching the earrings to the findings. For example, in this design the tab was drawn extending from the top of the figures' heads.

3. Make two copies of the design with the drawn tabs. Cut the designs out and glue them to the metal with rubber cement. This will give you a matched pair. You can also use two different but harmonious shapes rather than identical shapes for your earrings.

4. Carefully saw out the shape just outside the edge of the design (see tips on following page).

5. Using a fine-cut file, file and round the edges. This will give the earrings a more finished look.

6. Sand the edges first using the 600-grit sandpaper, then sand again using the 1000-grit sandpaper. For an even grain on the metal, sand in one direction rather than back and forth.

7. Using the round-nose pliers, make a loop from each tab by bending the tab backward while curving it over the jaw of the pliers. Make sure the loop you make is large enough to accommodate the jump ring.

8. Open the jump ring sideways and insert it into the loop you made from the tab. Close the jump ring.

9. Open the bottom ring on the French wire just enough to easily slip over the jump ring. After slipping it over the jump ring, close the ring on the French wire.

TIPS ON SAWING

Your first attempt at sawing can be a challenge. By following a few simple rules, it can become quite easy.

1. *When you attach the blade to the jigsaw, make sure it fits tight and that the blade's teeth are facing out and down.*

2. *Keep the blade in a completely vertical position when sawing.*

3. *Use even up and down motions when you saw. Turn the metal, not the saw, as you follow your pattern.*

4. *To turn a sharp corner, continue sawing in place as you turn the metal.*

5. *If you need to stop, loosen one side of the saw blade and remove it carefully.*

6. *It is best to saw on a bench pin. This is a rectangular block of wood that has a v-shape cut out of it. The wood, with the v-shape pointing away from the table, is clamped to the table using a C-clamp.*

7. *Lubricating the back of the saw blade (the side without teeth) with beeswax will help make the blade cut more smoothly.*

you did what?

Where were you when you got your ears pierced? A friend's bedroom, two ice cubes and a large safety pin— many of us share a variation of the same do-it-yourself experience.

Since the earliest piercings signalled an initiation, the shaman, elder, or priest performed the ritual. When barbers were also local surgeons, people came to them for minor operations, blood letting, and ear piercing.

Throughout most of history, ear piercing has been the job of midwives, nurses, and mothers. A simple home procedure often involved placing a cork behind the lobe that was then pierced with a sharp threaded needle. A loop was made by knotting the ends of the thread that passed through the ear. By gently pulling the loop through the hole daily, the hole remained open while it healed. Once healed, more substantial earrings could be inserted.

Today, easy-to-use ear piercing instruments make this a hygienic, quick, and almost painless procedure. Doctors' offices, jewelry shops, and beauty salons offer this service. After the piercing, a stud earring (a stone or bead on a post) is inserted. The post should be made of a hypo-allergenic metal (usually surgical stainless steel) to minimize the chance of an allergic reaction.

By rotating the earring while the hole heals, the hole will remain open. Cleanliness is essential for preventing infection. Applying rubbing alcohol or an antibacterial liquid to the piercing several times each day aids proper healing.

NATURAL and FOUND OBJECTS

Some of the best earrings can be made for the cost of a daily newspaper, some can be made for free. You can almost pick a pair of earrings off a tree or vine when you use natural materials. And while scouting yard sales, thrift stores, or flea markets, you can find interesting bits of costume jewelry or items with design potential.

DYAN MAI PETERSON
Gourd Earrings

MELANIE ALTER
Pottery Shards Set in Silver

Imagination is the greatest tool for making earrings out of natural and found objects. Look beyond the object itself and consider it for its potential design. What intrigues you about the object? Is it the symmetry, the color, or a special material that can be whimsically recycled. Select what you want to use, and if you can attach it to a finding, you can make it into a great pair of earrings.

LAVELL EVANS
Carved and Painted Gourds

SUSAN MOODY
Recycled Piano Keys

Tools and Materials

You'll need to be inventive when working with natural and found objects. What they're made of and the ultimate design for your earrings will help you determine what tools and materials to use. Begin by assembling the basics—pliers, wire cutters, head pins, eye pins, jump rings, wire, and findings—and go from there. As an example, perhaps an object will look better and be stronger if you use cord or leather rather than wire for stringing or hanging it. This should signal that you would need crimp coils to give you a loop.

What if the object doesn't have an obvious place for attaching a loop? Make one! Use an awl or hand drill to make a hole. Take into consideration the fragility of the material and act accordingly. You don't want to crack the object, so proceed with caution.

A MOTORIZED CRAFT TOOL may be a welcome addition to your workshop if an object is particularly hard to cut or drill. With extra attachments you can also sand, buff, and etch. Investing in this tool can provide you with years of use for a variety of projects.

WRAPPING WIRE is another way to make an attractive support, frame, or "cage" for holding your object and making a loop. Use two kinds of wire, copper and silver for instance, for a contemporary mixed-metal effect. Experiment with shapes of wire other than round such as square, triangular, or half-round.

BEADS, THREAD, AND NEEDLES can all be useful when working with natural and found objects. Use the thread to wrap the tops of objects (such as feathers) to give them a finished look as well as providing you with enough space for inserting a jump ring. Glue beads to a natural object to enhance the design. Sew an object to leather or fabric for extra support or as a design element.

JUDY MALLOW
*Pine Needle Weaving
with Teneriffe Center*

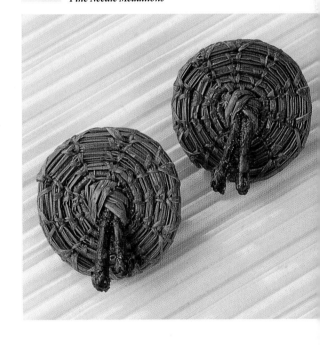

A STRONG, QUICK-DRYING GLUE will work on most materials. If you're incorporating paper, cardboard, or fabric, use white craft glue or white glue suitable for fabric. To protect natural materials, seal the earrings with spray varnish in a gloss or matte finish. Remember to avoid drips by applying two or three lighter coats, allowing each to dry before applying the next.

OTHER MISCELLANEOUS ITEMS you might find useful would be acrylic paints, artist's brushes, disposable foam brushes, metallic leaf, lint-free rags, and old newspapers to protect your work surface.

The best advice for working with natural and found objects is to be flexible and creative as you work. This may mean more uncertainty when starting a project, but it can lead to a unique pair of earrings that you will treasure.

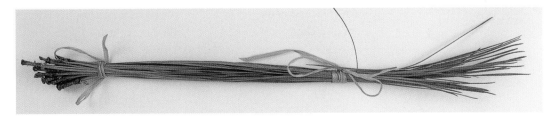

DESIGNER:
Dyan Mai Peterson

Mini-Gourds

Mother nature gave us a perfect blank canvas when she created the gourd. The surface of this dried fruit invites embellishment while the naturally round shape of these Japanese mini-gourds provides the inspiration for these hanging spheres.

MATERIALS

- Japanese mini-gourds— available at local farmers' markets, through gourd-supply catalogs, or grow your own!
- Leather dye in black, turquoise, and British tan— available at shoe repair shops, at craft shops, or through leather-supply companies.
- Clear satin-finish spray lacquer
- 2, 1-inch (2.5 cm) eye pins
- Beads
- 2 small sticks
- Quick-drying glue
- 2 fishhook ear wires

TOOLS

- Hobby saw with fine-tooth blades
- Pencil
- Wood-burning tool with small straight tip
- Motorized craft tool with small engraving cutter
- 3, 1-inch (2.5 cm) foam brushes
- Hand drill or awl
- Round-nose pliers

INSTRUCTIONS

1. If the outside of the gourd is not clean, use warm water and a stiff brush to remove the dirt and mold. Be careful not to scratch the surface.

2. Turn the mini-gourd on its side and very carefully cut the top off with the saw. When you have cut three-fourths of the way through the top, cut very slowly the rest of the way to avoid cracking the gourd.

3. With the pencil, draw three abstract squares around the top fourth of the gourd. Using the wood-burning tool, trace over the pencil lines. Do not burn too deeply, otherwise you may go right through the gourd.

4. Using one of the sponge brushes, paint the top part of the gourd with the black leather dye. Allow the dye to dry.

5. Next, using another foam brush, paint the inside of the square with the turquoise leather dye.

6. With the third foam brush, paint the rest of the gourd with the British tan leather dye. Allow the dye to dry.

7. Spray on the clear satin-finish lacquer. Several light mistings are better than one heavy coat which will make drips. Allow the lacquer to dry.

8. Draw three abstract shapes around the top of the gourd. Using the carving tool, carve out the abstract shapes.

9. Make holes on either side of the top of the gourd with the awl or hand drill. If you are working with a thin-walled gourd, do this carefully to avoid cracking the gourd.

10. String small beads of your choice on the 1-inch (2.5 cm) eye pin. Using the round-nose pliers, make a loop at the end of the eye pin.

11. Thread a small stick into one of the holes in the side of the gourd. Slip the eye of the eye pin onto the stick. Thread the stick through the other hole in the side of the gourd. Leave at least ⅛ to ¼ inch (.3 cm to .5 cm) of the stick extending from either side of the gourd. Trim the stick if it is too long.

12. Take two beads and glue them onto the ends of the stick extending from either side of the gourd. Put a few drops of glue on the stick where it touches the gourd on the inside.

13. Attach fishhook wires to the loop you made on the top of the eye pin.

DESIGNER:
Dyan Mai Peterson

Fanciful, Festive Dangles

If you like the look of larger, longer dangles but are afraid of the extra weight, try these lightweight earrings of tube beads made from gourds. With this design, you can turn up the volume when you're in a festive mood by adding as many strands as you want.

MATERIALS

- 5 Japanese-mini gourds—available at local farmers' markets, through gourd supply catalogs, or grow your own
- A variety of small beads
- 2 beads with large holes
- Leather dye in orange, medium brown, oxblood, and turquoise—available at shoe-repair shops, craft shops or through leather supply companies
- 2 fishhook ear wires
- 2, 1-inch (2.5 cm) eye pins
- Quick-drying glue
- Waxed linen thread in black

TOOLS

- Pencil
- Hobby saw with fine-tooth blades
- Small round file
- 4, 1-inch (2.5 cm) foam brushes—for applying paint (cotton swabs also work well)
- Awl or hand drill
- Needle-nose pliers
- Round-nose pliers

INSTRUCTIONS

1. If the outside of the gourd is not clean, use warm water and a stiff brush to remove any dirt and mold. Be careful not to scratch the surface.

2. With a pencil, mark guidelines on the neck of the gourd for cutting. A ³⁄₈-inch (1 cm) to ¹⁄₂-inch (1.5 cm) width makes a good-sized tube bead.

3. Using the saw and following your guidelines, cut the neck of the gourd into sections. Depending on the length of the gourd's neck, you should be able to get two to four "tubes" per gourd. Cut the gourds until you have 10 tubes (five per earring).

4. Clean out the inside of each tube, using the round file.

5. Color the tubes with the leather dye, using the foam brushes or the cotton swabs. For interest, you could make the outside of the tube one color and the inside another. Allow the dye to dry.

6. Using the awl or drill, pierce a hole through one side of each of the tubes.

7. Cut 10, 5-inch (12.5 cm) lengths of the waxed linen thread. Tie a small bead to the end of each of them.

8. From the inside out, insert the un-beaded end of the threads into the holes in the tubes. The beads on the inside act as anchors for the thread.

9. Taking your assortment of small beads, string them on the ends of the thread that extend from the tubes. Leave an un-beaded tail approximately ¹⁄₂ inch (1.5 cm) long on each.

10. Take an eye pin and two small beads, one slightly larger than the other. Thread the larger bead on the eye pin first, then the smaller one. Repeat on the other eye pin. By placing the beads this way, the larger bead will help cover the knot you will make in the next step.

11. Take five strands of thread that have the beads on them and loosely tie one large knot with all the ends. Do not tighten it. Take one of the large beads with the large hole and slip it over the knot. Open the eye of the eye pin and insert it into the center of the knot. Close the eye and tighten the knot. Repeat with the remaining five strands and eye pin.

12. Using the needle-nose pliers, bend the bottom of the eye pin, pushing it into the hole of the large bead. Add a few drops of glue and let the glue dry.

13. Using the round-nose pliers, make a loop on the end of the eye pin. Open the loop and insert the ear wires, then close the loop.

DESIGNER:
Lavell Evans

Imagine!

With gourds as your basic material, let your imagination take flight when envisioning all the different shapes you can create. For these earrings, designer Lavell Evans interprets the graceful look of butterfly wings and gives maximum impact to tailored geometrics. His advice, "Choose easy shapes, then focus on color!"

MATERIALS

- One clean gourd
- Fine sandpaper
- Oil pastels—available at craft or artist-supply shops
- Earring findings
- Strong glue
- Natural shellac in a can

TOOLS

- Pencil (and ideas!)
- Motorized craft tool with a circular-saw attachment
- Hand files
- Wood-burning tool
- Damp rag

INSTRUCTIONS

1. Design your shape. When you have one you are happy with, cut it out of the gourd using the craft tool.

2. Sand the backs of the gourd pieces. Using a fine file, file the edges of the pieces to remove any rough spots.

3. With a pencil, lightly draw your designs on the surface of the gourd shapes you've just cut. You can trace a design or draw free-hand.

4. With the wood-burning tool, trace over the pencil lines. Be patient, don't rush. The pieces are small and you don't want to burn through them. Then burn the outside edges of the pieces to give them a finished look.

5. When you have finished burning the design and the edges, gently clean the earring pieces with a damp cloth. Let them dry completely.

6. Before you apply any color, set the finding. Glue on an ear post or clip back. Take the time to let the glue dry thoroughly. This may take several hours, but you want the finding to be secure. If you are attaching ear wires, drill a small hole at the top, insert a jump ring and attach the wires.

7. Using the pastels, lightly apply colors of your choice to the designs. Because pastels are transparent on gourds, you want to use them to enhance the design embellishments rather than impart strong colors.

8. Carefully dip the earrings in shellac. Dip only the outside and sides of your earrings to give them a shiny patina. Avoid getting shellac on the findings. Let the shellac dry thoroughly; this usually takes one day.

DESIGNER:
Dyan Mai Peterson

Golden Gourds

Highlight your designs with gold for a dressier, designer touch. Because gourds are so lightweight, make your gourd earrings as big as you dare. If you're gluing a back to the earrings, either a post or clip, use a finding with a bigger pad to support the larger size.

MATERIALS

- Gourd
- Leather dye in British tan, black, and turquoise—available at shoe-repair shops, craft stores or through leather-supply catalogs
- Clear satin-finish spray lacquer
- 2 small sticks
- Beads
- Waxed linen thread in black
- Metallic gold pen
- 2 earring posts with 10mm pads, or 2 ear wires
- Strong, quick-drying glue

TOOLS

- Stiff scrub brush
- Hand drill or awl
- Small handsaw
- Grapefruit spoon-or any spoon with a serrated tip
- Pencil
- One piece of paper or cardboard
- Tape
- Fine sandpaper, 220 grit
- Wood-burning tool
- 3, 1-inch (2.5 cm) disposable sponge brushes
- Paper plate
- Motorized craft tool with an engraving attachment, or small hand-carving tool
- Round-nose pliers

INSTRUCTIONS

1. If the outside of the gourd is not clean, use warm water and a stiff brush to remove the dirt and mold. Be careful not to scratch the surface.

2. Use an awl or a drill to pierce a hole in the gourd. The hole should be large enough to insert the saw blade.

3. Insert the saw blade into the gourd. Cut the gourd in half in any direction, then cut the halves again, cutting the gourd into quarters.

4. Use a grapefruit spoon to clean out the inside of the gourd.

"Don't waste your gourd! The inside fiber that you remove can be used for making paper. You can plant the seeds or dye them with leather dye and add some beads and string them for a necklace. The seeds, high in fat and protein, make great bird and squirrel food."

—*Dyan Mai Peterson*

5. To make a template, draw the desired shape you want for your earring on a piece of paper or cardboard. You may want to make a pair of asymmetrical earrings by designing two harmonious shapes.

6. Tape the template onto the gourd surface and trace around the pattern with a pencil.

7. Using the handsaw, cut out the shape. Then cut a matching shape (or coordinating shape) for the second earring.

8. Clean the backs of the shapes. Sand the backs, fronts, and sides lightly with fine sandpaper.

9. Using a pencil, draw two horizontal straight lines ⅔ of the way down from the top of the earring, making them approximately ¼ inch (.5 cm) apart,

10. With a wood-burning tool, burn the pencil lines.

11. Using a 1-inch (2.5 cm) disposable sponge brush, paint the top portion of the earring with British tan dye. To cut down on the mess when using dyes, use paper plates for disposable palettes.

12. Using another brush, paint the area between the lines with turquoise leather dye. If you find this color too bright, add a little British tan dye to tone down the color to a more subtle and earthy hue.

13. Using the third brush, apply black leather dye to the bottom portion of the earrings. Let dry.

14. Draw small abstract shapes onto the bottom black portion of the earring.

15. Using the motorized craft tool with engraving attachment, carve the shapes. You can also do this using a small hand-carving tool or knife.

16. Using the metallic gold pen, trace the carvings. Let dry.

17. Seal the earrings with clear satin-finish spray lacquer. Apply three (or more) coats, allowing each coat to dry thoroughly before applying the next coat. Be careful not to spray too much lacquer in any one coat; it will run and create drips. The more coats you apply, the shinier your earrings will be.

18. Thread a small stick through a large bead. Use waxed linen thread to tie the smaller beads to the stick. Set aside.

19. If needed, sand the backs of the earrings to make them smooth. Apply black leather dye to coat the back and sides of the earrings. Be careful not to apply too much dye to the sides and back because it will absorb and soak into the carvings on the front side. (If the gourd is thin, you may want to use black spray paint instead of the dye.)

20. Take the beads and sticks and glue them to the turquoise areas between the two horizontal lines.

21. Glue the 10mm pad to the back of the earring. The larger pad will give you a larger gluing surface. If you are using ear wires, use the awl to make small holes at the tops of your earrings. *Have a gourd day!*

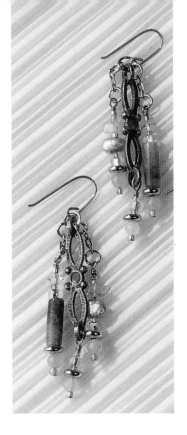

DESIGNER:
Cindy Vandewart

Instant Treasures
Using Recycled Jewelry Components

Make the most of interesting jewelry pieces found in thrift stores or at flea markets. A keen eye can spot components that will create beautiful new earrings with an antique touch. Dissect the old with your pliers, add some beads or charms, and you will have a unique treasure to add to your collection.

Triple Dangles

MATERIALS

- 2, 1-inch (2.5 cm) head pins
- Beads—this pair includes rhodonite tubes, 4mm aventurine, blue topaz chips and a variety of other glass and metal accent beads
- Recycled jewelry components
  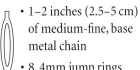
  - 1–2 inches (2.5–5 cm) of medium-fine, base metal chain
  - 8, 4mm jump rings
  - 2, 1½-inch (4 cm) head pins
  - 2, 1¼-inch (3 cm) head pins
  - 2, 5mm jump rings
  - Ear wires

TOOLS

- Round-nose pliers
- Flat-nose pliers
- Wire cutters

INSTRUCTIONS

1. String the beads on the 1-inch (2.5 cm) head pins. Leave approximately ½ inch (1.5 cm) at the top to wrap the wire and make a loop.

2. Attach your pieces of the recycled jewelry to the loops of the head pins. This will make two dangles. Set aside.

3. Take two lengths of chain ¼ inch (.5 cm) long—include at least three links—and attach the 4mm jump rings to both ends of each length. Set aside.

4. String beads on the 1½-inch (4 cm) head pins for one of the three dangles and make a wire loop as you did in Step 1.

5. Take the chains with the attached jump rings, open one jump ring and slip on the wire loop of one of the dangles you made in Step 4. Repeat on the other dangle.

6. Repeat steps 3–5, using 1¼-inch (3 cm) head pins to make two more dangles.

7. Open the 5mm jump rings sideways and insert all three dangles. Close the jump ring.

8. Attach to the ear wires.

"The trick for this type of earring is finding the perfect recycled jewelry component. Ask your aunt or grandmother if you can look through their old unwanted jewelry. Try yard sales, thrift shops, or antique shops. Look at large pieces for their components. My recycled pieces for the 'Granny's Necklace' earrings actually came from an old necklace of my grandmother's. It probably had a story, but unfortunately I never learned it."

—*Cindy Vandewart*

Granny's Necklace

MATERIALS

- 2, 1-inch (2.5 cm) head pins
- 6mm garnets and accent beads
- Recycled jewelry components
- Jump rings
- Ear wires

TOOLS

- Round-nose pliers
- Flat-nose pliers
- Wire cutters

INSTRUCTIONS

1. String the beads on the head pins for the bottom dangle.

2. Attach to the bottom of the recycled jewelry component using the wire loop technique.

3. Attach the dangles to the ear wire, using a jump ring if necessary.

Chinese Coin Earrings

MATERIALS

- 2, 6mm bloodstones
- 2, 4mm frosted fancy jasper
- Various other glass and metal beads
- 6 head pins in a variety of lengths
- 2 predrilled Chinese coins
- Jump rings
- Ear wires

TOOLS

- Round-nose pliers
- Flat-nose pliers

INSTRUCTIONS

1. String the beads on the head pins to make three matching pairs. Vary the placement of the beads and the length of head pins, keeping in mind their juxtaposition to each other. For composition and balance, the larger beads should be placed near the bottom of the head pin.

2. Attach each head pin to a hole in the Chinese coins.

3. Open the loop on the earring wire and attach to the coin, using a jump ring if necessary. Close the loop.

DESIGNER:
Susan Moody

Piano Keys Figures

Recycle piano keys that have been removed from old pianos because of wear or discoloration. You can ask piano tuners or your local piano shop if they have any. The ones pictured are old ivory, but old celluloid and plastic keys are also available. Since piano keys are approximately 1mm thick, you could substitute plastic, poster board, or thin wood for the figures.

MATERIALS

- Piano keys (or substitute)
- Rubber cement
- Masking tape
- Permanent inks
- Fine sandpaper
- Gesso
- Acrylic paints
- Gloss acrylic finish (matte if desired)
- 22-gauge sterling silver or copper wire
- Fine steel wool
- 2 jump rings
- 2 ear wires

TOOLS

- Jeweler's saw and fine saw blades, size 2/0 (You may also use a jigsaw with fine saw blades.)
- Bench pin
- C-clamp
- Fine small file
- Needle tool
- Small artist's paintbrushes
- Drill with small (size 50–55) drill bit
- Wire cutters
- Propane torch—these are inexpensive and easy to find at hardware stores. Follow the manufacturer's safety precautions. If you already have an acetylene torch, you can use it for this project.
- Pliers

INSTRUCTIONS

1. Design your figures so they are jointed for movement. (Almost like a rod puppet.) Take some time to plan how you want your figure to move and where you will place the joints to accomplish that movement.

2. Using the rubber cement, glue two keys together, back to back. By doing this you can cut two pieces at the same time— perfect for earrings. Allow the rubber cement to dry completely before proceeding.

3. Wrap the glued pieces with masking tape and transfer the design or shapes onto the masking tape. This process of gluing the pieces, then wrapping them adds extra strength when cutting.

4. You'll get the best results if you saw on a bench pin. It is a block of wood with a V-shape cut out of it. You fasten it to the workbench or table with a C-clamp. Using the jeweler's saw (or jigsaw) carefully saw around the outlines of your shapes or design. To avoid splitting the pieces, keep your saw blade in a vertical position and turn the pieces, not the saw, as you follow the design. When you finish, carefully unwrap your pieces and separate them where they were glued. If necessary sand or file any rough edges.

5. Before you paint, let the surface of the keys determine the technique you'll use for coloring the pieces. If the surface is smooth and shiny, you can etch the pieces with a fine needle tool, then color them with permanent colored inks, much like a scrimshaw technique. The bird earrings were done this way. Or, you can paint them with acrylic paints like the cats. To paint, first sand the pieces, then apply one or two coats of gesso before painting. Small brushes are perfect for adding detail, or you can also use small permanent markers. When you've finished painting, coat the surface with one or two coats of gloss acrylic finish (use a matte finish if desired).

6. Lay out your pieces to see where they will overlap, drill the holes for the joints accordingly. A good rule is to leave at least ⅛ inch (.3 cm) from the edge of the piece. Drill a hole at the top of each top piece of your figures for attaching the jump ring.

7. Take the small silver wire and cut enough 1½-inch (4 cm) pieces for all the joints in your figures.

8. Using the propane (or acetylene) torch, heat one end of each piece of wire until it "balls" up. Use heat-proof gloves and safety goggles while you work, following the torch manufacturer's safety precautions. When the wire cools, clean it with steel wool.

9. Thread one piece of the wire through two overlapping pieces (a joint) of your figure. Leave only ⅛ inch (.3 cm) of the wire extending out the back. You want the "ball" created by heating the wire to be on the right side of your figure. With the wire cutters, cut off any extra wire and, using the pliers, bend the end into a loop. Do this for all the joints in your figures. Make sure you leave enough space to hold the pieces together while allowing room for movement. This may take some practice, but eventually you will find the right tension to put on the wire—just be careful because too much tension can break the pieces.

10. Attach a jump ring to the top of each earring, then attach the ear wires.

DESIGNER:
Peggy DeBell

Bottle Cap Earrings

Designer Peggy DeBell made the green earrings for her 50th birthday. Each charm carries its own personal meaning. She found the items while browsing in bead and craft-supply shops, general merchandise stores, and even a fishing tackle shop.

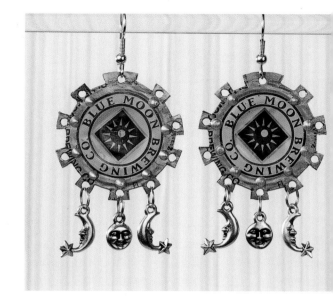

MATERIALS

- Recycled bottle caps
- Heavy fabric (approximately ½ yard (45.5 cm)
- Split jump rings
- Charms, old jewelry parts, etc.
- Assorted jewelry findings, wire, or beads
- French ear wires
- Dimensional "puffy" fabric paints

TOOLS

- Pliers (use good gripping pliers, not round-nose)
- Round-head hammer
- Small hand drill or small motorized craft drill
- Tin snips

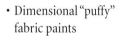

INSTRUCTIONS

1. Use pliers to pull out the "fluted" edge of the bottle cap.

2. Cover a hard surface, such as a sturdy workbench or tabletop, with fabric. The fabric should be about the weight of blue jean denim. Turn the bottle cap top-side-down and lay it on a hard, covered surface.

3. Using the round-head hammer, hammer out the edges until the bottle cap is flat. Start at one edge and work your way around the cap. Because you may need to practice this on several bottle caps before getting it right, save your favorite bottle caps until you've mastered this technique.

Note: At this point you can decide whether you want the cap to remain flat, like the green earrings, or to have cut edges, like the blue and red pairs. If you want it to remain flat, go to Step 5.

4. To make the cut edges, begin by turning the cap over so the top is facing up. Use the tin snips to cut the edge about every ¼ inch (.5 cm). Using the pliers, bend every other strip all the way around. You can either bend the strip forward (as in the red earrings) or back (as in the blue earrings).

5. Using a simple hand drill or small craft drill, drill holes in the top for attaching the ear wires and several in the bottom for attaching the charms, etc. For an added design element, you can drill holes in all the strips as in the blue earrings.

6. If desired, use the fabric paints to decorate the bottle caps.

7. Using the split jump rings, attach the charms to the bottle cap. Split jump rings have an extra round of wire like a key chain, providing an extra measure of security for the item you're attaching. They will not work open as standard jump rings do on occasion. You can use wire, beads, pieces of old jewelry, or purchased jewelry findings like chain links to extend the length of each dangle.

DESIGNER:
Judy Mallow

Pine Needle Zipper

If you want a quick introduction to working with pine needles, designer Judy Mallow leads you through the basics. When you're done, you will have learned how to prepare the needles, how to do a simple weaving technique, and how to make a great pair of natural earrings to wear and enjoy.

MATERIALS

- 2, 12-inch (30.5 cm) longleaf pine needles
- Artificial sinew or strong thread
- 2, 6mm bell cap
- 2 drop post findings

TOOLS

Scissors

INSTRUCTIONS

1. To prepare the pine needles, place them in a heat-proof container and cover them with boiling water. Let them soak for 30 minutes. Pour off the water and wrap them in a towel to "mellow" for about one hour.

2. Separate the pine needles into three sections or strips running the length of the needle as in Figure 1. Bend section 1 to the left.

4. Next, following Figure 2, bring section 2 over the top of section 1.

5. Bend section 1 to the right and back over sections 2 and 3 as in Figure 3.

6. Then bring section 3 over the top of section 1 as in Figure 4.

7. Repeat these steps over the length of the pine needle.

8. To adjust the length and size of the earring, either push the primary working section up to tighten the weave, or pull the section down to loosen the weave.

9. Loop the two ends of the pine needle together and tie with a sinew or strong thread. Trim both ends off closest to the knot. You may want to put a dab of glue on the knot to secure it.

10. Attach a 6mm bell cap and drop post.

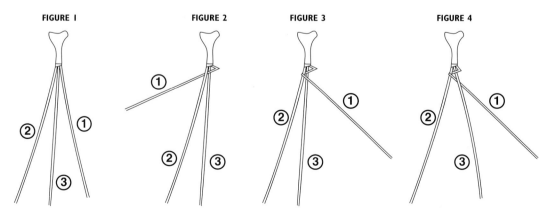

FIGURE 1   FIGURE 2   FIGURE 3   FIGURE 4

what about us?

Not everyone has pierced ears. At the beginning of the twentieth century there was a subtle shift away from ear piercing based on the changing times. One reason was that women were joining the work force and wanted to dress more professionally. Another was that pierced ears were considered old-fashioned, particularly in America as more immigrants became assimilated into a new culture. The trend continued to build for several decades until, in the late 1940s, it was considered almost barbaric for a woman to have pierced ears.

Even though piercing the lobe fell from fashion, women still wanted to wear earrings. Screw back findings were introduced in the early twentieth century, though not without their drawbacks. The mechanism could not support earrings with much weight, limiting the size and style of earring, and the screw backs would loosen, resulting in lost earrings.

It wasn't until the 1930s and the introduction of the clip back that women could wear larger, heavier earrings without piercing their ears. Many would claim this invention was a boon to fashion but a definite setback in comfort. As styles changed and earrings grew larger, stronger springs were needed to keep the clips on the lobes, making the earrings uncomfortable to wear for long periods of time.

DESIGNER:
Judy Mallow

Sometimes You Feel Like A Nut

Nature provides design inspirations in some of the simplest forms—spiderwebs, snowflakes, and sunlight through the leaves. If you're lucky, an idea may even drop into your lap. With black walnuts and hickory nuts, you can literally gather a great pair of earrings in no time.

MATERIALS

- Black walnut or hickory nut
- Shellac or clear acrylic spray

TOOLS

- Band saw, coping saw, or fine-toothed handsaw
- Sandpaper
- Rotary tool or electric drill with ¹⁄₁₆-inch (.16 cm) bit

INSTRUCTIONS

1. Using the saw, cut the nut to get two, ¹⁄₄-inch (.5 cm) (or less) slices. Clean the nut meat from the slice.

2. Sand both sides of the nut slice.

3. Drill a hole at the top edge of each nut slice.

4. Use the shellac or clear acrylic spray to coat both sides of the nut slices. Let them dry.

5. Attach earring findings.

Black Walnut End Cap Earrings

Use the end of the black walnut for a variation on these earrings. Use the same tools that you used for the sliced earrings to cut off the end of the nut. Drill a hole at the top. Sand the ridged side of the nut end to highlight the "radiating" design from the center. Coat both sides with shellac or clear acrylic, let dry, and attach your finding.

DESIGNER:
Judy Mallow

In A Nutshell

Is this a bedtime story in the making? The miniature basket made from a walnut shell is the perfect size for this little mouse. Spanish moss and bird seed complete his snug habitat.

MATERIALS

- 2 small English walnuts
- Shellac or clear acrylic spray
- Spanish moss
- Bird seed
- 2 small wooden mice
- 2, 6mm jump rings
- 2 drop post findings

TOOLS

- Rotary tool with cutter blade, or fine-toothed handsaw
- Sandpaper or sanding attachment for motorized craft tool
- Hot-glue gun and glue sticks

INSTRUCTIONS

1. Using the rotary tool or fine-toothed saw, cut each nut as shown in the diagram.

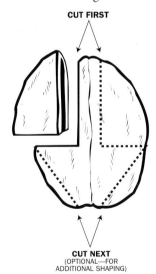

CUT FIRST

CUT NEXT
(OPTIONAL—FOR
ADDITIONAL SHAPING)

2. Clean out the meat of the nut and sand the cut areas smooth.

3. Use shellac or clear acrylic spray to seal the nut. Allow to dry.

4. Cut the Spanish moss into small piece. Put a small amount of glue in the bottom of the nut. Place a small amount of moss on the glue. Continue to layer the glue and moss until the nut is full.

6. Put a small amount of glue on top of the moss, then sprinkle with bird seed.

7. Glue the mice to the moss.

8. Spray the mice and bird seed with shellac or clear acrylic spray. Allow to dry.

9. Attach a 6mm jump ring to the handle of the basket. Attach the bottom loop of a drop post to the jump ring. Glue the jump ring to the bottom of the handle.

DESIGNER:
Susan Kinney

Once Broken, Forever Loved

Don't cry when you break a favorite piece of pottery. Smile at the thought of recycling the pieces into unique and beautiful earrings. Keep the design simple and remember to be mindful of the weight as you assemble your collage to avoid making earrings that are too heavy.

MATERIALS

- Assortment of broken thin pottery
- Paints for coloring the shards
- Cyanoacrylate glue, or strong, quick-drying glue
- Waxed linen thread
- Small glass beads
- Small flat brass beads
- Earring posts or clips

INSTRUCTIONS

1. Arrange small pieces of broken pottery into a pleasing collage. Using the paints, color the shapes and edges as needed. Example: paint all the edges black for a consistent appearance.

2. When satisfied, glue pieces together.

3. String small beads onto three pieces of waxed linen thread. Tie a small knot at the end of each and add dab of glue to secure.

4. Arrange the dangling strings under a flat brass bead on the collage and secure with glue.

5. Glue on the earring findings of your choice.

ACKNOWLEDGMENTS

MANY THANKS TO THE DESIGNERS FOR THEIR OVERWHELMING AND ENTHUSIASTIC RESPONSE TO THIS TOPIC. Their creative energy and technical support helped shape this book and reinforce the idea that earrings are, and will continue to be, universally loved. I especially appreciate knowing that so many light hearts are eagerly at work throughout the country and are attuned to the creative network—you make my job a delight. To Tricia Lindsay-Ramirez of Gallery of The Mountains in Asheville, North Carolina, for resource support. To Chris and Evan for an easy, enjoyable, and always enlightening shoot. To Orrin for his ability to see between the lines. To Daniel, Nina, and Jim for their patience and understanding. And thanks always to everyone at Lark Books for continued encouragement and support.

(TOP OF PAGE)

DYAN MAI PETERSON
Gourd Mask with Earrings

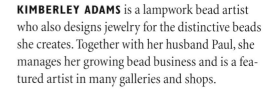

CONTRIBUTORS

KIMBERLEY ADAMS is a lampwork bead artist who also designs jewelry for the distinctive beads she creates. Together with her husband Paul, she manages her growing bead business and is a featured artist in many galleries and shops.

MELANIE ALTER is always designing new jewelry (and at present, some scarves and vests!). Her work has been shown around the world. Many of the charms, pendants, clasps, and buttons featured in her earrings come from her mail-order business *The Melanie Collection* (505) 298-7036.

BETTY BACON has been interested in fashion and art since childhood. She specializes in jewelry design using sterling silver or gold-filled wire combined with modern glass. She sells her jewelry through her company, *Treasured Designs*, in Chantilly, Virginia.

LORI BARTHOLOMEW is a polymer clay artist from Canton, North Carolina. In addition to her clay business, *Jewelry Designs by Lori Ann*, she is an interior decorator. She participates in numerous shows where she sells her work and demonstrates her craft.

PEI-LING BECKER has been developing many new artistic applications for paper and origami since coming to the U.S. in 1988 from the Republic of China. In addition to being a full-time studio artist, Pei-Ling teaches workshops and classes involving paper arts and crafts.

dj BENNETT, a former art and English teacher, devotes her creative energies to exploring textile art—primarily machine embroidery. In her classes, she stresses an active working relationship between fabrics, threads, and creative imagination.

MARJI BROHAMMER has always enjoyed dreaming up new ways of doing things and new color combinations. As a bead artist, she enjoys the time she spends planning and considering new projects because it always seems to lead her to many more.

JACALYN BRULL has a B.F.A. in metalsmithing from the University of Georgia and has attended Penland School of Crafts. Her work is currently being shown in Asheville, North Carolina, where she lives and works.

LINDA CHAPMAN believes her dance training continues to influence the movement in her work. She has shown her bead work in galleries around the country and is currently working on sculptural pieces that allow light to pour through them, making the beads come "alive."

IRENE DEAN is a full-time polymer clay artist living in the mountains of North Carolina. In addition to jewelry, she also creates functional and decorative objects for the home and office in polymer. She markets her work under the name *Good Night Irene!* through festivals, shows, specialty shops, and galleries.

PEGGY DeBELL has explored the possibilities of hand-painted and printed clothing and jewelry made of recycled materials for the past 13 years. Peggy has been a member of the Southern Highland Handicraft Guild since 1985. Her studio is in Asheville, North Carolina.

BARBARA ELBE has authored one book on amulet purse design and is currently working on the second one. She has also written two books on beaded earrings. She believes her background in oil painting and her work for the park system of northern California enables her to translate her love of art and nature to her bead work.

LAVELL EVANS began working as a gourd artist ten years ago. He has created his own approach to the use of pastel colors on gourds in addition to techniques for burning and sculpting them. He has exhibited his work across the country and lives and works in Bisbee, Arizona.

THERESA GUTHRIE currently is working and designing with beads and threads in weaving and braiding. She teaches classes in needle woven fiber jewelry and on-loom bead weaving. She has organized a large (and growing) bead exposition in the northeastern United States and is active in her regional bead society.

MARY SCOTT HOYT loves making jewelry. She is a preschool teacher who, in addition to working with PolyShrink, incorporates silver, paper, and friendly plastic material into her designs.

SUSAN KINNEY designs interiors, eclectic furnishings, jewelry, and raku pottery. She attributes the Oriental influence in her designs to having lived in Japan and Hawaii. Her business, *Suezen Designs*, in Asheville, North Carolina, can be reached at Designdr@circle.net.

JUDY MOFIELD MALLOW is a fifth generation basket maker and author of two books on pine needle basketry. She also runs her own mail order business, *Prim Pines* in Carthage, North Carolina, which provides pine needle basketry supplies to customers nationwide.

LEIGH McADAMS is a mixed media artist, working in cardboard, paint, paper, fabric, paper mache, metal, wire, yarn or whatever fits in a particular spot. She was a successful handweaver for 12 years but now is particularly interested in exploring block printing and marbling.

SUSAN MOODY teaches art to high school students in the Albuquerque, New Mexico, public school system. For the past ten years she has designed, made, and sold jewelry from old piano keys to stores and galleries around the country.

CAROL PERRENOUD makes small and intricate beadwork pieces that almost always involve some sort of "wee beastie" she has known or studied in her other career as a zoologist. She is a partner in a mail-order business, *Universal Synergetics' Beadcats* (503) 625-2323, which manufactures its own brand of Czech pressed-glass beads.

DYAN MAI PETERSON is a versatile, multitalented designer who currently works her magic with gourds—mini to mighty. She has a gourd design business, teaches gourd craft, is a basket maker, and runs her own mail-order bird-toy business.

LISA RANDALL has a B.F.A. in painting from East Carolina University where she also studied metal-smithing. She enjoys weaving and currently works as a craft retailer.

SHEILA SHEPPARD thrives on the experimentation and blending of many materials. She says she is continually inspired to work... or is it play? Her personal discovery of polymer clay "has released my spirit adventurer to yet another realm of possibilities."

ELLSWORTH "ED" SINCLAIR has written three books on wirewrapping and is currently working on the fourth. He has been a featured artist on the craft show circuit for more than 20 years. His interest in minerals led him to gem and mineral shows where he was introduced to wirewrapping.

FRAN STONE enjoys the contacts she has made in her second career as a direct importer of glass beads from Japan. After retiring in 1981, she worked for The Shepherdess in San Diego, California, where she had an opportunity or explore her creativity before settling on off-loom techniques with seed beads.

LYNN SWARD is a fiber artist who translates her love of fabric into her polymer clay designs. She is also a dollmaker, and creates mixed media sculptures and collages. She lives in Virginia Beach, Virginia, where she also maintains her studio.

THALIA TRINGO, a glass beadmaker and jewelry designer, works out of her Cambridge, Massachusetts, studio. She teaches beading and beadmaking and lectures and consults on jewelry and craft marketing. She is active in the Society of Glass Beadmakers and her local bead society.

CINDY VANDEWART has two daughters who are drawn to her home studio where they make lots of "cool" things—just like Mom. She makes beaded jewelry, which she sells to galleries and shops, using glass, semi-precious stone and bone beads, and recycled old jewelry parts .

SANDY WEBSTER currently is a full-time studio artist and workshop instructor in fiberarts throughout the U.S., Canada, and Australia. she specializes in mixed media works for the body and wall. She has been featured in numerous publications and she shows her work in national, juried exhibits.

KATE DREW-WILKINSON, a lampworker and bead jewelry designer, shows her work in many leading galleries and boutiques. She has written a book on wire work for bead jewelry and a book on developing a successful bead jewelry business.

DONNA ZALUSKY of Washington, D.C., shows her handmade lampworked glass jewelry in featured galleries, bead stores, and boutiques throughout the country. She specializes in custom orders and offers private lessons.

SUGGESTED READINGS

THE STUDY OF HUMAN ADORNMENT provides a fascinating look into our shared need to express our creativity by transforming the ordinary into the beautiful. Many books explore this topic. You'll find a good overview on the history of jewelry in Guido Gregorietti's *Jewelry Through the Ages* (American Heritage, 1969). *In Earrings: From Antiquity to the Present* (Rizzoli, 1991) authors Daniela Mascetti and Amanda Triossi document the changing styles of earrings throughout Western civilization including their cultural and social implications. Charlotte Wruck, in *Jewels For Their Ears—Why Earrings Are As Popular Today As They Were 1,000 Years Ago*, (Vantage Press, 1980) presents material about earrings from a broad world view using photos from many cultures to illustrate her text.

If you are interested in learning more about specific techniques you may want to consider these books. For beading, *Creative Bead Weaving* (Lark, 1996) by Carol Wilcox Wells will lead you though all off-loom techniques. Carol Taylor's *Creative Bead Jewelry* (Lark, 1995) is a fun and easy-to-follow book featuring 70 how-to projects. Also, Virginia Blakelock's *Those Bad, Bad, Beads* (Virginia L. Blakelock, 1990) provides clear and concise information to get you started. If you've been inspired to create your own, *Making Glass Beads* by Cindy Jenkins (Lark, 1996) is a thorough treatment of how-to lampwork.

For polymer clay, Leslie Dierks and Steven Ford will delight you with stunning gallery pieces and projects you can make in *Creating with Polymer Clay* (Lark, 1996). Leslie Dierks, in her *Creative Clay Jewelry* (Lark, 1994), presents how-to designer projects, many of which can be adapted to earrings.

If you want to expand your knowledge of working with metal *The Encyclopedia of Jewelry-Making Techniques* (Running Press, 1995) by Jinks McGrath offers an illustrated, comprehensive overview. For wire, books by Ellsworth "Ed" Sinclair, *Moods in Wire*; *Moods in Brass and Glass*; and *Contemporary Wire-Wrapped Jewelry* (E.E. Sinclair, 1994; 1996; 1997) present projects in wire wrapping. Kate Drew-Wilkinson, in her *Basic Wire Work for Bead Jewelry* (Kate Drew-Wilkinson, 1993), shows how to string beads on wire, how to create an effective design, and finishing techniques for a special touch.

You can learn more about working with gourds in *The Complete Book of Gourd Craft* by Ginger Summit and Jim Widess (Lark, 1996), and about working with pine needles from Judy Mallow's *Pine Needle Basketry* (Lark, 1996).

INDEX